The Educational Conversation

SUNY series,
The Philosophy of Education
Philip L. Smith, editor

The Educational Conversation
Closing the Gap

Edited by
James W. Garrison
Anthony G. Rud Jr.

State University of New York Press

Published by
State University of New York Press, Albany

For information, address State University of New York Press,
State University Plaza, Albany, NY 12246

Production by Cynthia Tenace Lassonde
Marketing by Theresa Abad Swierzowski

Library of Congress Cataloging-in-Publication Data

The educational conversation : closing the gap / James W. Garrison,
    Anthony G. Rud Jr., editors.
        p.   cm. — (SUNY series, the philosophy of education)
    Includes bibliographical references (p.   ) and index.
    ISBN 0-7914-2447-2 (alk. paper). — ISBN 0-7914-2448-0 (pbk. :
alk. paper)
    1. Teachers—United States.   2. Teaching—Moral and ethical
aspects. 3.Education—United States—Philosophy.   I. Garrison,
James W., 1949-   . II. Rud, Anthony G.   III. Series: SUNY series
in philosophy of education.
LB1775.2.E35   1995
371.1'02—dc20   94-28369
                                                                          CIP

Contents

Foreword

The essays in this volume are unusual. They are intended to fill a gap in educational conversation, and they do so quite admirably. Educational conversation, at the state and national policy levels, overflows with talk of mathematics and science, test scores, outcomes, performance assessments, and opportunities to learn. Meanwhile, teenagers kill one another, children bear children with little or no resources to raise them, and kids ingest anything predicted to give them a buzz. In such a climate, it is good to widen the educational conversation to include topics such as luck, relational authority, irony, style, emptiness, privacy, and hospitality in the classroom.

The choice of topics is all the more interesting because it comes from a group of philosophers who have all done distinguished work in the analytic tradition, and their contributions here show the value of that training. However, not so many years ago, such training often included an admonition that certain topics and ideas were best left to everyday conversation and speculative writing. Striving conscientiously for the rigor encouraged by Bertrand Russell, analytic philosophers in education confined themselves to the analysis of concepts thought likely to yield to such treatment. For a while, there was a very real danger that philosophers of education would withdraw from the immortal conversation and settle for playing sophisticated linguistic games at the periphery of educational life.

Now, rejecting both nihilism and foundationalism, many philosophers are using their analytical skills and ironic voices to explore topics and questions central to education and to life itself. The contributors to this volume have decided boldly to reenter the immortal conversation. They dare to speak of the soul, longing, wisdom, tragedy, relation, and connection in teaching. Setting aside talk of subject matter lessons and tests, they draw frequently on teachers whose greatness did not depend on the scores their students made on achievement tests: Socrates, Jesus, Gandhi. They remind us that the eternal questions center on moral life, and that moral life is the heart of education. These essays invite readers to participate in a larger, more generous educational conversation. Reading them should produce a hunger for further exploration and still wider conversation. With luck and perseverance, that conversation may widen to include today's school children.

Nel Noddings
Stanford University

vii

Preface

This volume attempts two related though distinct tasks. It is a contribution to the growing body of literature on what Goodlad, Soder, and Sirotnik (1990) have called "the moral dimensions of teaching." In our introductory chapter, we point out our indebtedness to this literature. For our second task, we are on less familiar ground. We have attempted to capture it in terms such as "wisdom beyond knowledge" or the "non-rational" elements of the teaching and learning situation.

We are not rejecting rationality and celebrating the irrational. We do reject a narrow conception of rationality that still has strong currency in our culture, and particularly within teacher education. This narrow conception of rationality keeps the cognitive and evaluative elements of teachers' experience separate. Our authors develop a vocabulary consonant with a rationality that is responsive to practical contexts and values. In doing so, we combat two powerful cultural dogmas that have conspired to hold the cognitive and moral apart.

First, we follow Dewey (1929; 1984) in calling for abandoning "the quest for certainty." For Dewey, the world was rife with chance and incompleteness. Our classrooms, like our lives, are always fragile places. Rules and principles have a place, for relative stability also characterizes this world. Yet such rules and principles do not have an abstract, indubitable, and timeless quality. Luck and chance have a role in life and in teaching and learning. In chapter 2, Shirley Pendlebury notes that one aim of the modern science of teaching is "luck diminishment." She argues that it is futile and inhumane to banish luck from teaching and learning, much less any human endeavor. Luck stands in the way of the quest for certainty.

Second, we follow many others in rejecting the distinction between fact and value. Many educational theorists and researchers still hold that rational inquiry and cognitive judgment tell us the way the world *is*, while moral judgment suggests how the world *ought to be*. In our introductory chapter, we examine the prominent research of Lee S. Shulman and his associates, and show how Shulman tends to uphold the distinction between fact and value.

Reasoning is never detached from values. Dewey sometimes called human beings "thinking desire" to underscore that emotions, moral action, and values could *not* be separated from rational thought.

Champions of the quest for certainty believe rationality is a factory for producing laws, rules, and principles. Our authors reject such merely technical senses of rationality as dangerously incomplete. If by rationality one means that logic is an intellectual tool detachable from practical contexts and values, then our authors reject rationality. If one sees rationality in coping with uncertainty while attempting to realize what is *morally possible* within the world, then our chapters are rational. The goal of these chapters is to *cope* with the practical challenges of life in classrooms rather than attempt futilely to *copy* the dictates of some timeless truth.

This volume seeks to contribute to a conversation about teaching and learning rather than conclude a study or treatment. These chapters are reflective occasions for those who seek wisdom beyond knowledge. None of our authors dictate "performance standards" or the like, but they do challenge the reader to think hard about what to value and believe in teaching and learning.

The first chapter sets the context for what follows. We treat in some detail recent discussions of the moral aspects of teaching and learning. We show how our volume contributes to this topic in a fresh and distinct way. Some readers may prefer to construct their own contexts. We encourage them to sample the selections in this volume before returning to read what we, as editors, thought was one interesting introductory context among many. We welcome comments from such readers.

Shirley Pendlebury explores the themes of luck, fragility, and contingency that the second and third chapters of our collection assume in their analysis of the tragic and ironic dimensions of teaching. For Pendlebury, teaching, like any particular and context bound practice, "is a lucky business." In some ways "openness to luck" in teaching is good fortune. It provides for serendipity, creativity, and growth. It is good to seek systematic knowledge in order to free teachers from "blind dependence on what happens." The danger for Pendlebury comes when the desire to totally eliminate the nonrational, as opposed to the irrational, yields to the elimination of teacher judgment, choice, and therefore, responsibility.

Nicholas Burbules recognizes the "tragic dimension of teaching" that arises out of the exercise of authority in classroom contexts. There is only "limited time" to deal with goals that have "mutually incompatible consequences" or "consequences we can never know" and processes that are often "completely beyond our influence." Burbules develops a notion of authority in teaching that recognizes this tragic element and stresses the importance of relationships and dialogue.

The chapter by James Garrison explores the possibilities of an aesthetic response to the fragility and contingency of teaching through the development by teachers and teacher educators of an individually creative style. Such style operates in the gaps that must be left by even the best scientific research on teaching. Style, like science, arises out of the acknowledgment that "chaos and anarchy are with us." Science can only go so far in providing guidance to the teacher in a timebound practical context. When reductive science tries to eliminate uncertainty individual creativity is destroyed. Garrison connects style as a moral virtue to democratic social relations among teachers, administrators, university researchers, and policy makers, and argues near the end of his chapter that bad science also destroys democratic social relations by distorting communication. He reminds us that etymologically logic derives from dialogue (literally to speak or say) and dialogue is best sustained by democratic participation.

Alven Neiman champions the "ironic temper" characteristic of many great moral teachers like Socrates and Jesus. For Neiman, complex irony "aims at a new understanding beyond the conventional meanings of our words and deeds" and beyond the discursive categories of the technocratic "experts." On the surface, Neiman concedes "complex irony presents obvious falsehood; but in its enigmatic presentation it points towards a deeper reality." That is why Neiman thinks that we should "make irony into a major virtue to be taught to inhabitants of an ideal liberal democracy."

The very title of the chapter by Leonard Waks, "Emptiness," is a challenge to the "reductive scientific studies, and nature dominating technology, at the center of the educational enterprise." Waks examines Socrates, Jesus, and Gautama the Buddha as paradigmatic "masters and teachers of the art of living." All three have the ability of "exposing the irrational foundations" of our lives that, ironically, we believe are rational. Emptied of our irrational "craving" for excessively abstract and reductive "rationality" we are ready to truly learn through "a *rational examination* of our delusions."

Sophie Haroutunian-Gordon begins by acknowledging that "the word 'soul' occurs but rarely in contemporary educational discourse." She sees this situation due to "the science of psychology" and remarks that "modern educational theories have been constructed upon the stories provided by modern psychological theory." Haroutunian-Gordon's concern is with "turning the soul." She follows through on the Platonic suggestion that dialogues redirect the soul, and proceeds to analyze actual classroom exchanges that are logical enough, but not in the technician's sense. The goal of such teaching is to illuminate the "brightest regions of being" where "truth" may be discerned. Truth here is not some detached scientific proposition corresponding to the objective "facts," but the kind of interpretive insight and understanding that comes to those who listen well.

C. J. B. Macmillan turns our vision inward with "Some Thoughts on Privacy in Classrooms." He begins with the observation that "classrooms are public places" and is concerned with the status of privacy therein. Macmillan takes a paradoxical turn when he defends the conclusion that "privacy is a social practice" that creates moral persons. This way of thinking confounds the discursive practices of scientistic educational researchers who assume dualistic categories of private vs. public and subject vs. object. Macmillan concludes by exploring the practical "classroom payoffs" of viewing privacy as necessary to the creation of moral persons.

Anthony G. Rud Jr. evokes an ethos of hospitality in teaching and learning by first taking us with him into a Benedictine monastery. There we learn the importance of "the achievement of a hospitality toward and knowledge of oneself. Hospitable acts create an emptiness that would then allow the world and strangers to speak to oneself, and one would be able to listen and hear them." Rud contrasts this sharply with what Foucault (1979) calls disciplinary technology where "growth in learning and spirit is frequently sacrificed for an accumulation of grades, credits, and other badges of merit." He concludes by inviting us to consider the kind of practical hospitality fostered at his former workplace, The North Carolina Center for the Advancement of Teaching (see Rud and Oldendorf, 1992).

Earlier versions of chapters 3, 5, and 7 were presented at a symposium chaired by Anthony Rud at the annual meeting of the American Educational Research Association in 1992. We would like to thank Gary Griffin, program chair, for inviting us to this session, and Daniel Liston for his role as critic. A version of chapter 9 was presented at the annual meeting of the American Educational Studies Association in 1992. We are indebted to many colleagues and friends for insight and conversation as we worked on this volume. Tammie Smith and David Starkey of Virginia Tech gave talent and expertise in the preparation of the manuscript. Lois Patton of SUNY Press encouraged this project through difficulties and uncertainties. We would like to acknowledge the helpful criticisms of the following students: John Abrahams, Howe Bachman, Nancy Ballinger, Lois Berlin, Jacquelyn Boddie, Sheila Carter, Norm Crane, Patricia Devitt, Becky Domokos-Bays, Linda Fore, Laura Goad, King Godwin, Daisy Goodwin, John Hamel, Betty Hobbs, Marsha Jackson, Hester Jones, John Krysa, Susan

McCartney, Joanne Moche, Leslie Murrill, Sue Stevens, and Jim Washington. Floating on the New River, second oldest in the world, gave respite and inspiration over several days of intense discussion and editing. Finally, we give thanks to KSL and Rita for their love and support during this long project.

JWG	AGRjr
304 WMH	School of Education
Virginia Tech	Purdue University
Blacksburg, VA 24061-0313	West Lafayette, IN 47907-1440
(703) 231-5598 (W)	(317) 494-6542 (W)
wesley@vtvm1.cc.vt.edu	rud@sage.cc.purdue.edu

We look forward to hearing from you.

CHAPTER 1

Introduction

_____ *James W. Garrison and Anthony G. Rud Jr.*

The rhetoric of current educational reform divides the events of the past decade and a half into two or more "waves." First-wave reports like *A Nation at Risk* (1983), *Making the Grade: Report of the Twentieth Century Fund Task Force on Federal Elementary and Secondary Education Policy* (1983), and *Action for Excellence* (1983) connected education to economic competitiveness and the necessity for a more productive workforce. Business and industry saw students as means to their ends. These reports and their supporters sought to improve education by emphasizing greater external specification and technocratic control of school processes and especially school products. The key concept was "accountability"; that in practice meant standardized testing and performance evaluation. Students would have to pass state mandated tests for prizes such as "literacy passports" that allowed promotion and graduation. Teachers would likewise face state mandated behavioral proficiency examinations modeled after the pioneering Florida Performance Measurement System. Several seminal works on educational reform and its history (Callahan, 1962; Tyack, 1974; Wise, 1979; 1988) criticized similar actions when instituted years before these latest reforms.

We are now a decade into the "second wave" of educational reform initiated in the middle 1980s by organizations such as the National Governors' Association (1986), The Holmes Group (1986), the Carnegie Task Force on Teaching as a Profession (1986), the Education Commission of the States (1986), and The Public Information Network (1985). The second wave reform literature has flooded the field with calls for enhanced teacher professionalism and empowerment connected to restructured schools where teacher participation and collaboration are encouraged. Decentralized democratic schools and teacher professionalism are the new panaceas.

Actually, it is not clear which wave of reform we are in. Some, such as Goodlad, Soder, and Sirotnik (1990), see the second wave beginning

1

with *A Nation at Risk* in 1983. Others consider the decentralization of school administration as a third wave. It does not matter; many teachers and teacher educators now feel that they have been thoroughly soaked. We wonder if it might not be time to generate a new wave from the paradoxical clashes of the nonrational and ethical components of practice with scientific analysis.

Each successive wave of school reform washes turbulently over the one before. Reformers have revised requirements for accountability but the clarion still resounds. The Holmes Group's *Tomorrow's Teachers* (1986) talks about "the transformation of teaching from an occupation into a genuine profession" (p. ix). Yet as David F. Labaree (1992) notes "words such as *examination, standards,* and *certification* appear fifty-seven times in the first section of the report" (p. 637). Labaree believes the document is redolent of "scientistic rhetoric and the voice of the expert" (p. 630). Labaree finds the rhetorical appeal of a science of education to be potentially dangerous for two related reasons:

> First, rationalized constructs cannot capture the complex ways in which schools work. Good teaching is inherently unrationalizable, since it must be responsive to the peculiarities of time and place and to the need of individual students; general rules just do not prove very helpful to teachers in the day to day decisions they must make in classrooms. . . . Second, the effort to intervene in schools on the basis of these scientific constructs is inherently antidemocratic. It elevates the university expert over the classroom practitioner and the citizen, and it effectively removes schools from popular control by transforming them from a political problem (amenable to democratic process) into a technical problem that can be solved only by those with the necessary specialized knowledge. (p. 632)[1]

A central theme of our book is that the contemporary educational conversation is dominated by a technocratic ideology that either denies the existence of particularistic, time-bound and unrationalizable components of concrete classroom practices, or ignores them.

The work of Lee S. Shulman (1987a; 1987b) has contributed heavily to a great deal of second wave rhetoric regarding teacher professionalism and empowerment. Shulman attempts to construct "the teaching knowledge base," that, once "codified," contributes to "the concept of a National Board of Professional Teaching Standards" (see Shulman, 1987a; 1987b). Obtained by studying expert teachers, this "codifiable" knowledge base then may be used in the schooling and testing of those learning to teach.

Shulman (1987a) enumerates "at least four sources for the teaching knowledge base" (p. 8). The last of these four, "the wisdom of practice itself," provides a particularly wide window into his program:

> The final source of the knowledge base is the least codified of all. It is the wisdom of practice itself, the maxims that guide (or provide reflective rationalization for) the practices of able teachers. An important task for the research community is to work with practitioners to develop codified representations of the practical pedagogical wisdom of able teachers. (p. 11)

We claim in our book that recognition of the nonrational aspects of teaching requires an acceptance of the insight that some very important elements of excellent practice are *not* codifiable.

It is hard, however, to disagree with Shulman (1987a) when he says that "one of the frustrations of teaching as an occupation and profession is its extensive individual and collective amnesia, the consistency with which the best creations of its practitioners are lost to both contemporary and future peers. . . .It is devoid of a history of practice" (pp. 11–12). For Shulman "a significant portion of the research agenda. . .involves the conducting of 'wisdom-of-practice' studies" (p. 12). There is important work to be done here, but we note that Shulman's notion of wisdom contrasts sharply with that of John Dewey.

For Dewey the moral domain was not entirely distinct from the cognitive. We should not be surprised then by the following claim by Dewey:

> . . .rigid moral codes that attempt to lay down definite injunctions and prohibitions for every occasion in life turn out in fact loose and slack. . .No elaboration of statute law can forestall variant cases and the need for interpretation *ad hoc*. . .The only truly severe code is the one which foregoes codification, throwing responsibility for judging each case upon the agents concerned, imposing upon them the burden or discovery and adaptation. (1922; 1983, p. 74)

We believe that many of the most important acts of teaching begin not with acts of reason, but where rational principles and sound reasoning fail. Such contexts are by definition nonrational. The purpose of rational inquiry is to reestablish rationality by reconstructing our principles and habits in ways that work. Ironically, such situations are often strokes of good luck disguised as bad. They prod us to offer hospitality to different or novel principles and persons who then may help us build better habits. For Dewey, effective action and inquiry often calls for "wisdom beyond knowledge."

Shulman (1987a) seems to limit wisdom mostly, if not entirely, to forms of rational knowledge when he writes:

> As we have come to view teaching, it begins with an act of reason, continues with a process of reasoning, culminates in performances of imparting, eliciting, involving, or enticing, and is then thought about some more until the process can begin again....we will emphasize teaching as comprehension and reasoning, as transformation and reflection. (p. 13)

Such a conception of the activities of teaching, while robust, does ignore some important dimensions. We shall argue in more detail later that such a view creates *a moral gap* in the educational conversation about teaching and teacher education.

In a response to Shulman, Hugh Sockett (1987) identified just such a gap and suggested that Shulman's research rhetoric might be the scientistic voice of the expert.[3] Sockett finds Shulman's strategy flawed in four ways. First, there is its lack of attention to context. Comparing expert golf to teaching, Sockett notes "context, personality, temperament, and style are not merely adjuncts to the knowledge base; they are the very stuff of practice....Indeed, uncertainty, variability, and contextual and individual uniqueness give the game its particular charm, allure, and addictive quality for player and spectator alike" (p. 209). Second, its language is inadequate to describe the moral framework of teaching. Third, it lacks a sophisticated account of the relation between reason and action in teaching. Finally, Sockett sees the first three flaws rising out of the fact that "Shulman's analysis appears assessment-driven" (p. 208). These criticisms parallel Labaree's points made about second wave reform rhetoric.

Sockett states that "the paratechnical language...will not meet Shulman's aspirations for detailing the complexity of good teaching. Too many researchers want to use a language that can provide objective statements about human behavior in teaching which is drawn from the scientific paradigm" (pp. 211–212). As a result, Sockett, commenting on Shulman's analysis of the expert pedagogue Nancy, observes:

> What is so unsatisfactory about these descriptions of Nancy? Briefly, they represent an attempt to describe (dispassionately) Nancy's *technique*....What all this fails to describe, because the language is so limited, are Nancy's *moral virtues* as a teacher. Ultimately, the observer is left mumbling with an inadequate

language of description in the presence of excellence, grace, economy, style, enthusiasm, commitment, integrity, care, passion, and a sense of fairness, because she does not have, or dares not use, a moral language. (p. 211)

The absence of a moral language in which to theorize, describe, and research teaching is, perhaps, the greatest gap in the contemporary educational conversation. The gap is even more striking when one thinks about one's own teaching. Outside the boundaries drawn by someone's research agenda a moral vocabulary about teaching is pervasive. The intellectual and cognitive biases of most educational researchers contrast sharply with considerations of moral and aesthetic elements that so often preoccupy classroom practitioners.

Shulman (1987b) recognizes that the moral dimension of teaching is important: "surely, teaching is a moral activity, an activity made meaningful because of the goals pursued and not only the means employed....Sockett's insistence that we more explicitly add a moral dimension to such analyses is wise and well grounded...there is a socio-moral quality to teaching, but it is only one of many essential qualities" (p. 477). Yet Shulman makes his own preferences unquestionably clear when he states that "I have always held that my first obligation as a scholar is to describe and explain with such clarity that my readers can render their own moral judgments" (p. 476). This passage flirts with the old positivist separation of facts from values. Although Shulman realizes that it is untenable, one can almost hear him longing for it. He asserts a cognitive and intellectual line of inquiry preferred by second wave theorists, researchers, granting agencies, and policymakers.

All of the essays in our volume display alternative nontechnical vocabularies concerned with the particular and often unrationalizable components of concrete practice. If recognized and allowed into the conversation, these components could help the second and third waves of reform soak into the field of classroom practice. The chapters of our book confront the nonrational aspects of teaching that lie beyond the limits of even the most refined scientific knowledge. We do not mean to suggest that these essays are a celebration of the irrational. They are a careful and insightful investigation of what is to be done beyond the limits of certain knowledge. Each displays carefully wrought reasoning, discursive categories, and analysis of the particular situation, as well as what is to be done about it. These essays are thought provoking, challenging, and often frustrating precisely because they represent "gaps" in the conversation. In fine, they are philosophical in the ancient Greek sense of the term *philosophia*, or "love of wisdom."

In an essay significantly entitled "Philosophy and Democracy," John Dewey (1919; 1982) opts to conceive philosophy as an alternative to "even the most demonstrated of scientific truths" (p. 43). Dewey (1919; 1982) states his alternative understanding this way:

> Put baldly, it is to deny that philosophy is in any sense whatever a form of knowledge. It is to say that we should return to the original and etymological sense of the word, and recognize that philosophy is a form of desire, of effort at action—a love, namely, of wisdom; but with the thorough proviso...that wisdom, whatever it is, is not a mode of science or knowledge....it is an intellectualized wish, an aspiration subjected to rational discriminations and tests, a social hope reduced to a working program of action, a prophecy of the future, but one disciplined by serious thought and knowledge. (p. 43)

Our authors seek wisdom beyond the limits of knowledge alone. They deal with the luck, tragedy, irony, style, emptiness, soulfulness, hospitality, and respect for privacy required to realize "the good" in teaching, the values of the practice. Since, though, they express their social hope as an intellectual wish, they subject it to rational discriminations and tests. They do not, however, assume some predetermined timeless canon of rationality. Sadly, scientistic rhetoric sometimes does attempt to sit in final judgment over classroom practice where those who fail the test are severed from the service while others just burn out.

The prevailing paradigm of research on teachers remains social science. Such research is characterized by anonymity, objectivity, and detachment. When we look at or experience the everyday work of teachers, we find particularity, emotion, and engagement. Teachers do not often recognize themselves in much current research. They are largely silent and feel devalued. A moral vocabulary enables us to see how teachers are engrossed in a task that involves their whole being in the development and exercise of practical wisdom and enlarges our conception of what a teacher is and does. The turn toward the emphasis upon a teacher's mind, away from teacher behaviors, has been led by theorists such as Lee Shulman, Hugh Sockett, and others. We would like to go a step further beyond cognition, and sometimes even moral principles, to the creative and free acts and products of an intellect exhibiting practical wisdom.

Our appeal is to the reflective practitioner who thinks hard about teaching. Again, we turn to Dewey (1919; 1982):

By wisdom we mean not systematic and proved knowledge of fact and truth, but a conviction about moral values, a sense for the better kind of life to be led. Wisdom is a moral term, and like every moral term refers not to the constitution of things already in existence....As a moral term it refers to a choice about something to be done, a preference for living this sort of life rather than that. It refers not to accomplished reality but to a desired future which our desires, when translated into articulate conviction may help bring into existence. (p. 44)

Wisdom *is* a moral term. All of the essays in our volume deal in one way or another with moral issues, but they do so in a way different from most. The space these essays help map is the difference between the *actual*, that which is or what some unimaginative people call reality, and the *possible*, what could and perhaps morally *ought* to be. The law of this unnecessary difference is legislated by agents of hegemonic power who constrain the wisdom of practice to their scientistic prescriptions. Expert knowledge is often translated into the power of control and domination through accountability measures, tests, and "observation" instruments.

We draw our vocabulary from ordinary life in and out of classrooms, though our discussion at times is philosophically complex. The loss of these words from our vocabulary about teaching further suggests how a dominant discourse cannot only be dehumanizing but self-alienating.

In using everyday terms for the moral life, we attempt to answer a common criticism of academic writing. Many teachers and teacher educators do not read research. Researchers frequently write to each other, and often eschew discussion that would inform practice. A restoration of everyday moral language to the dialogue about teaching and teacher education is needed. One way we can make such a restoration is by presenting a moral vocabulary *and* a philosophical justification. Ethics attempts to answer troubling questions concerning our relations with other human beings. The contributors to this volume are all concerned in one way or another with relations between students and teachers that comprise the moral dimensions of teaching.

Our volume suggests, through a study of the moral vocabulary of teaching, "gaps" in the larger moral conversation of our culture.[2] We ally ourselves more directly with some recent work dealing with ethics and teaching in this broader context. The most successful attempt to bring the ethical regions of teaching to the forefront of attention in the second and third wave debates over teacher professionalism and empowerment is *The Moral Dimensions of Teaching* edited by John I. Goodlad, Roger Soder, and Kenneth A. Sirotnik (1990). Their primary concern is with the preparation of teachers in schools and colleges of education. In their preface the editors query the untimeliness of their own text:

> But why a book of this nature at this time? Questions about virtue and moral character—not only of individual but of institutions—were perhaps more central to academic and public conversation several decades ago than they are now. . . .When it comes to institutions of higher education, there appears to be an increasing tendency to label such matters "purely philosophical" and relegate them to esoteric niches in the graduate curriculum. (p. xi)

Five of the ten contributors to that book are philosophers of education and all of the contributors to our own volume are also philosophers of education. There is no good reason that such a central everyday concern of teachers and teacher educators should be shunted off to the side in teacher education or be left to "only philosophers" to fuss over. There is a great deal of very hard and important thinking needed by practitioners, researchers, and theorists alike, and we all need to talk with each other more than we do.

In his chapter "The Occupation of Teaching in Schools" Goodlad (1990) joins the chorus of those who complain that the question of moral context is mostly ignored by the waves of reform documents, and provides what may be the ultimate response to Shulman's wisdom of practice research program conceived largely as a cognitive enterprise:

> Even if a well-developed science of teaching were available, its mastery by teachers would not provide sufficient guidance for the burden of judgment they carry, its full definition would not adequately frame a profession of teaching, and teacher education programs based on only this science would be seriously deficient. Virtually all of teaching in schools involves values and is guided by normative principles. (p. 19)

Eventually wisdom is beyond scientific understanding alone. It is as Dewey put it, "not systematic and proved knowledge of fact and truth, but a conviction about moral values, a sense for the better kind of life to be led" (Op cit.).

In the concluding chapter of *The Moral Dimensions of Teaching* Kenneth A. Sirotnik (1990) asserts "the commitment to rational thought—to nurturing and exercising the capability of human inquiry—is an implicit assumption underlying each of the contributions to this volume" (p. 298). The idea of that volume is a reflective ethics that connects "thinking" to "doing" as "envisioned long ago by Dewey" (p. 299). Dewey held the role of thinking and knowledge in moral action, or what he called "reflective morality," in the highest regard (see Dewey, 1932; 1985).

Yet wisdom, including moral wisdom, that is, "a conviction about moral values," or the good, is something that "refers not to accomplished reality but to a desired future which our desires, when translated into articulate conviction may help bring into existence" (Op cit.). There is a gap between the values that we strive to realize, the goods that we seek to bring into existence, and some actual state of affairs, such as facts revealed by scientific research on teaching. This gap defines a dialectical tension between the actual and the possible, what *is* and what morally *ought* to be.

We propose a vocabulary to discuss the moral good, to help fill and close the gaps in the educational conversation about teaching and learning. Ultimately, we are drawn in our reflections on the practice of teaching to the tragic, ironic, often private existential questions about what it means to be human and to be in relationship to other humans. Answers to these questions, if there are any, lead us to recognize a more subtle gap in teaching. There is an essential, nonrationalizable, and ineluctable dialectical tension that accompanies moral actions. The chapters in this volume seek to identify, to rationally examine, or at least to intelligently reveal, aspects of this tension.

CHAPTER 2

Luck, Responsibility, and Excellence in Teaching

Shirley Pendlebury

How far is teaching a matter of luck? We would like to say not at all, or at least not to a significant extent. For if teaching is simply, centrally, or substantially a matter of luck, on what grounds may we praise or blame teachers for their work, in what sense can they be held accountable? And how could programs of teacher education make any difference to the effective practice of future teachers? Where luck commands, nothing is certain. It undermines the basis of our moral judgments and of our plans and predictions.

In any case, the question about luck and teaching seems inappropriate. "Luck" is not a familiar term in scholarly discourse or in the journals of educational research. "Luck" has its place in folklore, in narrative, in gossip, and in lame excuses. Think of some common conceptions of luck and related conceptions like fortune and chance. Two of them are often personified: Lady Luck and the goddess Fortuna. Fortuna has the power to distribute the lots of life according to her humor. Her emblem is the wheel and it betokens vicissitude. Unlike Justice, Fortuna is neither even-handed nor consistent. Like Luck, she is courted with charms and offerings yet she may if she pleases spurn her most devoted courtiers in favor of those who have spurned her. There is no controlling Fortuna: she belongs in the mythology of wanton and fickle women. When things go badly for us, we blame bad luck or ill fortune; when they go well for others, we envy their luck or good fortune.

These are some of the ways we talk or think about luck in our gossip or our daydreams. But to talk this way—indeed to talk of luck at all when we are trying to understand how and why practitioners fail or succeed—is like talking about magic. Luck-talk, like magic-talk, surely has no place in rational discussion.

This is one way of looking at it. There is another. Recent philosophical work by Martha Nussbaum (1986), Bernard Williams

11

(1981), and Thomas Nagel (1979) reminds us just how much our lives and practices are vulnerable to luck. Much of what we are and what we do is a consequence of luck or contingency—of what is beyond our control because it is not brought about by our own agency. In her rich and provocative reading of Greek tragedy and philosophy, Nussbaum (1986) argues that the very things that are most important for a flourishing human life—friendship, love, politics, and health—are deeply vulnerable to reversals of fortune.

Much of what Nussbaum says about human life in general is applicable to the human practice of teaching. Both the richness and the importance of the practice are due, in part, to factors over which we should not want complete control. Were we to succeed in excluding luck from teaching, we should do so at the expense of those deep and surprising insights that come to teachers and students who are able, when the occasion demands, to relinquish control. Serendipity is as precious in teaching as it is in science, in invention, and in exploration.

But teaching is not just a matter of luck; it is a public practice in which some people are put into the hands of others for specific purposes, usually at public expense. If we have no grounds for holding practitioners responsible for their work, if it is all just a lucky business, then the practice must lose credibility and public money spent on it can be little more than a gamble. We want assurance that it is possible for teachers to have the knowledge, skills, and personal qualities necessary for fulfilling the constitutive purpose of teaching—that is, to bring about or facilitate learning. For these and related reasons, the drive to protect practice from luck is strong.

Yet, if Nussbaum is right, it is neither possible nor desirable to exclude luck from practice. The question for educators is how to ensure the possibility of wise and accountable practice in the face of luck. Or, to borrow terms from an ancient Greek debate, it is a question about how far *techne* can safeguard the practice of teaching and its distinctive goods from *tuche* (or contingency), and a question about the kind of *techne* best suited to the task.

The *technai* were the gifts of Prometheus to naked and helpless humans to enable them to progress against contingency. Ship-building and shoemaking, flute-playing and sculpture, weather-forecasting and medicine were among them—a range of practices variously covered by our terms "art," "craft," and "science," all terms that have been used in modern times to describe the practice of teaching. Broadly defined, *techne* is

> ...a deliberate application of human intelligence to some part of the world, yielding some control over *tuche*; it is concerned

> with the management of need and with prediction and control concerning future contingencies. The person who lives by techne does not come to each new experience without foresight or resource. He possesses some sort of systematic grasp, some way of ordering the subject matter, that will take him to the new situation well prepared, removed from blind dependence on what happens. (Nussbaum, 1986, p. 95)

This is a formal rather than a substantive characterization of *techne*; it leaves many important questions open. The question of which kind of resource and foresight will best prepare a practitioner is debatable; so, too, is the question of what constitutes a systematic grasp of the subject matter.

For the Hippocratic doctors of old there were four interdependent features in virtue of which medical *techne* could defend practice from luck: universality, teachability, precision, and explanatory force (Nussbaum, 1986). Universality and precision together yield the possibility of true predictions about future cases and the possibility of explaining each case and treating it on the basis of systematic explanation and not simply on an *ad hoc* basis. Universality also yields the possibility of teaching because *techne* can be communicated in advance of experience. New practitioners come to each case prepared with the knowledge of general laws, established on the grounds of precise measurement and fidelity to the data. All four features bear upon the goal of mastering contingency.

"Luck" is a rare term in the extensive literature on teacher education and teacher reform. Nonetheless, much of the debate can be characterized as one about how best to diminish luck and thus ensure a sound basis for practice. During the twentieth century two strong luck-diminishment projects have been especially detrimental to teaching: one rooted in Frederick Taylor's science of management and a commitment to social efficiency (Taylor, 1911; Bobbitt, 1913; Callahan 1962), the other rooted in the empirical sciences (Gage, 1963; 1978). Both share much with the Hippocratic conception of *techne* and both have resulted in questionable research projects, in misconceived programs of teacher education, and in distorted notions of excellence and accountability in teaching. Contemporary wisdom of practice studies (Shulman, 1987) and attempts to formulate an epistemology of practice (Schön, 1983; Sockett, 1989) are all premised on a wariness of the promises of technical conceptions of science, management, and pedagogical reasoning. Their conception of *techne*, Sockett's especially, is more consistent with commonsense perceptions of the mutability, incommensurability, and particularity of practice.

These are strong claims. A full defense of them is well beyond the scope of a single chapter. My chapter has three main aims: To outline very roughly the ways in which teaching is vulnerable to luck; to sketch two luck-diminishment projects and their failures; and to examine some more promising ways of ensuring sound, responsible teaching despite the fragility of practice.

Teaching is a Lucky Business

Thomas Nagel (1979) provides a useful framework for categorizing the ways in which teaching is vulnerable to luck. He defines four categories of moral luck: Constitutive, circumstantial, causal, and consequential. Luck invades teaching in all four categories. Before saying why, let me define the categories.

Physical characteristics, temperament, and special abilities (or disabilities) are all matters of *constitutive luck*. They are those features of our constitutions that set limits on what it is possible for us to be and to do. Freckles, breasts, impatience, and musicality are examples. Some of my constitutive features I have in virtue of being human; I share these with other humans but not with cats, elephants, or angels. Some I have in virtue of being female; I share these with other females—both animal and human—but not with males. Some I have in virtue of being the child of my parents; I share these with some other members of my family. And some are special to me—they distinguish me from other humans, from other females, and from my parents and siblings.

Circumstantial luck concerns the circumstances in which we find ourselves at different times of our lives, and in particular the problems and situations we face. In so far as we can control or change circumstances, they are not a matter of luck. But there are many over which we have little or no control. The time, country, class, and community into which we are born are not chosen but given. I may choose to leave my country and my community; I cannot choose to leave my times. Some of the circumstances we find ourselves in are determined by history, others by nature. Some present us with opportunities for brave or just action, others do not. Yet without such opportunity, the courage or justice of which we believe ourselves capable make no difference to our moral records for, as Nagel reminds us, we judge others for what they actually do or fail to do, not just for what they would have done if circumstances had been different.

Causal and *consequential luck* have to do with the causes and effects of action. Causal luck concerns the way in which we are determined by previous actions or events, consequential luck with the way in which our projects turn out. I may choose to become a teacher—or join a revolution or live in abject poverty while I write the great South African novel—in the belief that this is what I am cut out for. Yet it may turn out, after much expenditure of the relevant currency (time, energy, passion) that I am a hopeless failure. This is a matter of consequential luck. In retrospect, I have to say I made the wrong choice, even if I choose for what at the time appeared to be the right reasons.

Both the practice of teaching and its primary and secondary agents—teachers and students—are open to luck in all four categories. Teaching is open to both *constitutive* and *causal luck* in three dimensions: In the talents, temperaments, personalities, and life histories of its primary agents; in the talents, temperaments, personalities, and life histories of its secondary agents; and in the way the practice itself is constituted.

This third dimension has to do with the history of teaching and with its cultural and institutional circumstances. Alasdair MacIntyre (1981) argues that practices and the institutions that sustain them characteristically form a single causal order in which the cooperative care for the common goods of the practice is always vulnerable to the competitiveness of the institution. If practices and institutions do form a single causal order then an institution's vulnerability renders the related practice vulnerable as well. Where school systems have been corrupted by abuses of power and status, where their material resources have been diminished by poverty, waste, mismanagement, or official theft, the practice of teaching must suffer accordingly.

The way in which the practice of teaching is constituted, and the understanding that different agents have of it, are partly matters of *circumstantial luck*. But unless students and teachers have a degree of common understanding of teaching and its aims, standards, and procedures, the practice is frustrated. To give just one example: the former policy of apartheid in South Africa generated not only a system of racially segregated schooling but also a system of epistemically different schools and universities. Rote learning was the norm at schools under the control of the Department of Education and Training (DET), which had been responsible, under apartheid law, for black education. Students who have learned from school experience that memorization and regurgitation yield good examination results are baffled and angry when they move from DET schools to educational institutions that put a premium on independent thought and argument.

Teaching is also vulnerable to *consequential luck.* As teachers we cannot be certain of the outcome of our actions. In formal terms, teaching is successful when a teacher succeeds in fulfilling her intention, say, to bring about understanding. But having the intention and acting on it are no guarantee of its fulfillment. Teaching, like selling, is a transitive activity with a double object: I cannot teach unless I have something to teach and someone to teach it to. In selling, success is more clear-cut than in teaching; a shopkeeper has immediate and obvious evidence of the end accomplished. Not so with teaching. While a teacher can ascertain through on the spot quizzes, tests, and assignments that the students have learned what the teacher has attempted to teach them, the teacher cannot be certain that the learning will be permanent. By tomorrow, or next Friday, or next January it might all have been forgotten or confused or distorted.

In any case, the mere presence of teachers and students in a classroom is an insufficient condition for teaching. Drawing from Aristotle's examples, Nussbaum (1986) identifies two ways in which luck may impede practice. First, circumstances may deprive an activity of some crucial instrumental means or resource. Secondly, they may deprive an activity of its object or recipient. In either case, the deprivation may be temporarily constraining or so complete as to impede the activity altogether. A medical doctor who has no access to the tools of the profession will be severely constrained in the treatment of patients; whereas one who has been deprived of knowledge (say by extensive memory loss) will be incapable of practicing at all. And a doctor with extensive knowledge and full access to a wide range of medical equipment cannot practice without minimally co-operative patients. Similarly with teachers. Under conditions of student resistance or refusal, it may not be possible to sustain the practice at all—as black South African teachers discovered, again and again, during a decade or more of student resistance to apartheid education.

I have sketched some of the ways in which luck—good and bad—comes into play in teaching. The openness of teaching to luck raises important questions about accountability and standards of excellence. Are we to abandon these requirements in the face of luck? Most emphatically not. But, as I shall argue, accountability and excellence in teaching are not to be accomplished by attempting to make the practice wholly safe from luck. The argument begins by looking at two strong luck-diminishment projects and their failures; one from the first half of this century, the other from the second.

Efficiency and Luck Diminishment

In modern times, one attempt to minimize luck in teaching has been especially ill-conceived and threatening to the vigor and integrity of practice. Behind it is the driving idea that if people, resources, and time are efficiently managed, practice will be well protected against contingency. For those who responded to the lure of Frederick Taylor's *The Principles of Scientific Management* (1911), efficiency was regarded not only as the criterion for industrial productivity but also as the ultimate moral standard by which public practices and institutions were to be judged (Callahan, 1962; Tom, 1984). Neither efficiency nor effectiveness is a despicable attribute. They are among the enabling conditions for human flourishing and for the flourishing of practices and institutions. But the application of Taylor's system beyond the factory floor had some unhappy consequences.

Perhaps the most notorious case in education was Franklin Bobbitt's application of the principles of scientific management to schools and teacher education. Bobbitt regarded education as "a shaping process as much as the manufacture of steel rails" (Bobbitt, 1913). For the process to result in a product of quality, it was necessary to specify standards for the product. Through the adoption of standards and related scales of measurement, educational administrators could "know with certainty" which principals and teachers were in need of help from the central office.

The stress on certainty, technically conceived standards, and measurement are typical features of attempts to make human practices safe from circumstantial and consequential luck. In addition, Bobbitt was prepared to take few chances with constitutive luck. As far as possible, major decisions were to be removed from teachers, who might be constitutionally unsuited to making and carrying out the right decisions. Not only were teachers to have nothing to do with the setting of standards, they were to have little or nothing to do with deciding on the best methods for their teaching. This would be "too large and complicated" a burden "to be laid on the shoulders of teachers" (Bobbitt, 1913).

Bobbitt's ideal was to give "absolute certainty" to the selection, training, and placement of teachers. On the basis of activity analysis, he asserted that all that was necessary for effective teacher-training was to

. . . list the two hundred or five hundred or five thousand tasks which the competent teacher accomplishes in his work. The

abilities to perform these tasks, then, are the fundamental
teacher-training objectives...(Bobbitt, 1913, p. 85)

This assumes, falsely, that the activity of teaching can best be
understood, and improved, by atomizing it into so many discrete tasks.
A similar assumption informs the stress on teacher "behaviors" in
performance-based teacher education programs and teacher
performance evaluation systems of more recent times, both of which
are allied to contemporary versions of the social efficiency tradition of
teacher reform (Macmillan and Pendlebury, 1985; Zeichner and Liston,
1990).

Bobbitt and other efficiency experts aimed to protect practice from
luck not by providing teachers themselves with methods and
procedures for taking control of crucial parts of practice, but by removing
control from them and placing it in the hands of administrators. By
restricting the people entitled to make crucial decisions, efficiency
experts in education hoped to protect teaching from inappropriate,
contradictory, unproductive, and wasteful decisions—all of them
invitations to luck. But by removing control from teachers, the primary
agents of teaching, the efficiency experts also undermined the ground
for excellent and accountable practice. There are two conditions under
which it makes no sense to praise or blame teachers for their work:
the first is where luck has free reign and the second is where the attempt
to exclude luck removes teachers' control over what they do and thus
their responsibility for what they do. Excellent practice is not possible
under either condition.

Science and Luck-diminishment

In the first half of this century much of the effort to protect teaching
from luck was predicated on the assumption that there is one best way
to teach and that the task of educational research is to find it (Tom,
1984). Bobbitt's work heralded a host of subsequent attempts to develop
teacher training programs that could be relied upon to produce effective,
efficient teachers. Although in the second half of the century researchers
in the process-product tradition have operated off less simplistic
assumptions about the nature of teaching; they are still concerned and
are working to establish which teaching methods can be relied upon
to effect learning. In their drive for reliability and precision, process-
product researchers turned—with increasing sophistication—to the chief
Promethean gift to humankind; the *techne* of measurement and
statistical analysis.

Both in conception and in intent the process-product research paradigm (Gage, 1963; 1978; 1983) meets all four of the ancient Hippocratic criteria for an effective *techne*: universality, teachability, precision, and explanatory force. Like the Hippocratic doctors of old, process-product researchers aimed to develop a systematic practice based on universal laws that provide an antecedent grasp of how to deal with new cases. The establishment of universal laws makes *techne* teachable in principle. Measurement ensures precision and fidelity to the data, crucial requirements for the predictive and explanatory force of general laws. Finally, to ensure the explanatory force of theory, research aims to establish causal connections between effective teaching and learning in much the same way as medical research aims at establishing causal connections between effective treatment and cure.

These, very roughly, are the ways in which process-product research has sought to protect teaching from luck. It has failed. Despite (or perhaps because of) its insistence on precision and measurement, the project has yielded no universal laws with any bite. Even if it had succeeded in this respect, there remains the problem of translating research findings into practice. The failures of process-product research are not only empirical and practical; conceptually it is deeply flawed (Doyle, 1978; Ericson and Ellett, 1982; Macmillan and Garrison, 1988).

But no matter how flawed the research paradigm and no matter how dismal its results, its driving idea contains an important truth: it is possible to study practice empirically. To deny this is to affirm what Macmillan and Garrison (1988) call "an abhorrent conclusion," namely that "the attempt to learn from experience is doomed for the start" (p. 2). Here, surely, is a luck-supremacy view. If it is impossible to learn from experience, we must always be taken by surprise, coming to each new event unprepared. Under conditions such as these, accountability and excellence are empty notions and any trust the public puts in teachers' work is ill-founded faith.

The question, then, is not whether it is possible to study teaching empirically but how and with what end in mind. One of the things we know from experience is that sometimes teaching brings about learning and sometimes it does not. If practice is not to be thoroughly undermined by skepticism, we must assume that when teaching accomplishes its ends this is not simply luck but is connected with the teacher's own efforts. Given this assumption, the question arises as to which kinds of effort are fruitful and which are fruitless. The task of research is to identify the conditions under which teaching is most likely to be fruitful. If these conditions are established with some certainty (by corroboration at least), they can serve as a foundation for teacher education programs and so ensure that teachers are in a position to fulfill their professional obligations without the risks incurred by intrusions of luck. This, very roughly, is the rationale for process-product research.

At the start of this section I sketched some parallels between process-product research and the Hippocratic conception of *techne*. It is time now for a more detailed picture. I draw my picture from Gage's *The Scientific Basis of the Art of Teaching* (1978).

The very title of the book indicates the kind of *techne* that process-product research hopes to develop. Gage's quest is not for a science of teaching but for a scientific basis for the art of teaching. His quest is not for luck-exclusion but for the systematic diminishment of luck's influence on practice. In the process-product research tradition the central strategy for luck-diminishment is the establishment of causal laws in teaching: "We search for 'processes'. . .that predict and preferably cause 'products. . .'" (Gage, 1978, p. 69). But however successful this search, luck-exclusion is impossible as Gage himself recognizes. Even if research could yield a full complement of laws concerning the non-chance relationship between teaching and learning, it is still up to individual teachers to judge when it is appropriate to act in accordance with a law and when not.

Judgment, for Gage, is one of the central features of art as opposed to science. Since teachers can be mistaken in their judgment of when it is appropriate to act in accordance with one law rather than another, it is at the point of judgment that luck can intrude on practice—for better or worse. Thus, reading Gage from the perspective of luck, we might say that the artistic dimensions of practice render it vulnerable to luck in ways which science cannot exclude.

A second reason why process-product research cannot exclude luck from teaching is that in practical affairs "the laws and trends relating to any two variables are subject to modification by the influence of. . .many more variables" (Gage, 1978, p. 18). Gage concludes that:

> . . .the scientific base for the art of teaching will consist of two-variable relationships and lower-order interactions. The higher-order interactions between four and more variables must be handled by the teacher as artist. (Gage, 1978, p. 20)

So limited a scientific basis may seem to be not worth having. Gage defends it on the grounds that "it is better to have generalization to which exceptions can be made than to have no generalization at all" (Gage, 1978, p. 20). A limited scientific basis is better than none because in the absence of general laws, practice has no informing *techne* and so consists of little more than a series of *ad hoc* maneuvers always exposed to the winds of fortune.

The quest for luck-exclusion is futile. Nonetheless, Gage's writing suggests that the influence of luck on practice can be diminished in two ways. Science provides the primary defense in the form of *techne* for practice. The secondary defense lies in what Gage calls "artistry"— knowing when and when not to follow scientifically established laws, generalization, and trends.

I want to look very briefly at some conceptual difficulties that lie at the heart of its failure to provide an appropriate *techne* for teaching. Once again, I focus on Gage's work. For educationists who want to improve teaching, Gage argues, the relationship between process and product is crucial. If one way of teaching is demonstrably better than another, we have a basis for training teachers and for improving teaching. If not

> . . .we are left without a scientific basis for the art of teaching. Then every teacher must use his or her personal common sense, intuition, insight, or art, with no guidance from any relationships or regularities that may have been laid bare through scientific methods. (Gage, 1978, p. 24)

Notice that Gage presents two mutually exclusive alternatives. Either science can provide a basis for teaching or it cannot. If it can, practice is accessible to systematic improvement and—by implication—to systematic protection from luck or contingency. If it cannot, the quality of practice is contingent upon the personal common sense, intuitions, and insights of individual practitioners and thus—again by implication—remains deeply vulnerable to luck. Here is a clear contrast between a firmly grounded *techne* and the absence of one; between having the generalizations and causal explanations which, Gage assumes, make systematic practice possible and teachable, and not having them. Without them, we must simply trust that teachers' common sense will be adequate for their task.

But this picture is distorted. In making too crude a distinction between art and science, Gage mistakenly assumes that only science, as conceived in process-product research, can offer a *techne* for teaching. This is not so. *Techne*, you will remember from the broad formal definition given earlier in this chapter, yields some control over *tuche* (luck) by providing us with "some sort of systematic grasp, some way of ordering the subject matter" that will take us into new situations properly prepared with foresight and resource, "removed from blind dependence on what happens." On this broad, formal conception, *techne* permits, but does not require, the kind of scientific basis that Gage and his colleagues are after. Which kinds of resources and which kinds of principles will provide practitioners with a systematic grasp of their practice, are open questions. They do not have to be answered by statistical analysis of correlations between teacher "behaviors" and student outcomes. Instead, they might be answered in the style of Lee Shulman (1987) by conducting qualitative studies of wise practice, or in the style of Alan Tom (1984) by developing a notion of teaching as a moral craft, or in the style of Donald Schön (1983), and Hugh Sockett (1989) by charting an epistemology of practice.

The point here is that there are alternate ways of giving substance to the notion of a *techne* of teaching, alternate ways of protecting practice from luck. Gage's picture is distorted not only in the limited range of alternatives it assumes but also in its view of art. Art, when it is meaningful, is not just a personal private matter. Like science, it is a human practice and like all significant human practices it has public goods, standards, and procedures which are shaped, understood and, within broad limits, shared by a community of practitioners.

Wise Practice in the Face of Luck

In 1987, *The Harvard Educational Review* carried an important debate on teacher reform in the United States (Shulman, 1987a, b; Sockett, 1987). It was important not only because it addressed issues of immediate concern to people involved in the so-called new reform movement— and those critical of it—but also because it raised issues of perennial and universal concern for the practice of teaching: those central epistemological and moral questions that call for reconsideration whenever a practice is in crisis, whenever it appears not to be fulfilling its characteristic ends, and whenever it appears to have lost sight of its internal goods and standards. The two contestants were, and still are, influential figures in educational circles: Lee Shulman, known for his work on knowledge in teaching, and Hugh Sockett, known for his work on teaching as a profession.

As I shall show, their debate can be characterized as one about how far teaching can be made safe from luck and about which conception of *techne* is appropriate for the task. The fact that Shulman and Sockett do not themselves use the terms luck or *techne* does not discredit this procedure. If the procedure yields a perspicuous account of the points at issue it will have accomplished its purpose.

I begin by outlining Shulman's "intellectual strategy" for reform in teaching. If professional reform is to be effective, Shulman argues, it requires both an epistemological foundation and an account of wise practice. Reading Shulman's intellectual strategy from a luck-perspective, two points are worth noting. First, an appropriate epistemological foundation provides practitioners with a systematic grasp and so helps to remove them from "blind dependence on what happens." Secondly, the stress on wise practice suggests the importance of judgment, choice, and responsibility. Luck-diminishment is not to be accomplished through the blind following of rules or procedures derived from the epistemological base.

According to Shulman, four main sources of professional knowledge provide the necessary epistemological foundation: (1) scholarship in the content disciplines; (2) "the materials. . .of the institutionalized educational process" (for example, textbooks and curricula); (3) research on schooling, learning, teaching, and "other social and cultural phenomena that affect what teachers can do;" and (4) the wisdom of practice. The last of these sources is elusive. Unlike law and medicine, teaching has no established case literature. Much of Shulman's energy has been devoted to filling this gap. Under the banner "wisdom-of-practice studies," he and a group of colleagues have undertaken the task of recording instances of teaching and teachers' reflections on them for the purpose of establishing a case literature of teaching practice and "codifying its principles, precedents, and parables" (Shulman, 1987a, p. 12).

Shulman sees teaching as an activity characterized by an ongoing cycle of comprehension, transformation, instruction, evaluation, and reflection. Teaching, he believes, is typically initiated by some text to be understood, where "text" is meant in the broadest sense to cover any material which students are required to or want to understand. Pedagogical reasoning thus begins with the teacher's comprehension which should, ideally, be relational and involve both the particular "texts" to be taught and their relation to other "texts" in the same field. In addition, the teacher must transform content knowledge (the text) into "forms that are pedagogically powerful" and adaptive to the variations in the students' abilities and backgrounds. The stages of comprehension and transformation are followed by the stage of instruction, the teacher's performance in the classroom which, in quality and manner, is dependent on the quality of the teacher's comprehension and transformation of the text for the students concerned. Two forms of retrospective reasoning—evaluation and reflection—follow instruction. Finally, as a result of reflection, a new comprehension is reached which is both retrospective and prospective.

The strength of Shulman's intellectual strategy for teaching reform is that it acknowledges the importance of the teacher's subject knowledge and judgment in good teaching—matters too frequently ignored or sidelined in luck-diminishment projects that are rooted in naively conceived quests for efficiency or effectiveness.

Sockett argues that the strategy is flawed in three respects: first, in stressing the content of teaching at the expense of its context; second, in the poverty of its descriptive language which fails to capture the moral dimensions of teaching; and third, in its account of the relationship between reason and action in teaching (Sockett, 1987). Before looking in more detail at some of the points at issue between Sockett and Shulman, it is useful to locate Sockett's criticisms in the context of his interest in developing an epistemology of practice—a prerequisite, he believes, for the improvement of teaching.

In a later paper Sockett (1989) lists six criteria for a sound epistemology of practice: (1) it should contain a view of truth and meaning; (2) it should find its primary reference point in action; (3) its account of rationality must be capable of articulating the variety of ways in which reason and action are related in teaching—*per hoc* reasoning (or what Schön calls reflection-in-action) is crucial; (4) it must acknowledge that teaching is an interpersonal and moral enterprise; (5) it must have a rich language of description, justification, and explanation; and (6) it must not depend on a scientific view of objectivity.

Sockett's criteria for an epistemology of practice constitute a non-instrumental *techne* of teaching. His central concern is to give an account of what is involved in a systematic grasp of the requirements of excellent and responsible practice, without falling into the traps of technicism. In his view, the particularity and unpredictability of teaching means that excellence cannot be characterized in terms of general, universal rules. Consider what he says, by way of analogy, about excellent golfers:

> It is "why they do what they do when" that characterizes. . . excellence: in particular, how they achieve that extraordinary unity of physical skill and judgment against the background of psychological tensions to which all players are subject. Context, personality, temperament, and style are not merely adjuncts to the knowledge base; they are the very stuff of practice. More puzzling about excellent players is the range of error, the misjudgments, and the sheer mistakes they make; that make us cautious of predicting success in golf and make us acutely aware of the game's unpredictability. (Sockett, 1987, p. 209)

The important question here is not whether excellent players play differently under different circumstances—for one of the marks of excellence is the capacity to respond appropriately to the circumstances—but rather how players come to acquire the "extraordinary unity of physical skill and judgment" which makes them excellent.

This surely is also the question that lies at the heart of Shulman's wisdom-of-practice project, whatever its flaws. How do novice teachers become experts? In other words, how do they acquire that extraordinary unity of skill and judgment which experts are able to exercise in diverse circumstances?

One of Sockett's challenges to Shulman's intellectual strategy is that in its stress on content, it ignores the uniqueness of each teaching situation and so cannot explain how experts acquire the skill and judgment necessary for responding to diverse circumstances. The point at issue is akin to the ancient conundrum about luck, *techne*, and the good life: If each new situation is truly unique, how can we ever have a comprehensive understanding of practice? In truly unique situations we cannot bring ourselves prepared to find features we have already grasped. We are, as Nussbaum (1986) says, always taken by surprise. If we can have no comprehensive understanding of practice, if there are no common features to be grasped in preparation for new situations, then how can practice be taught? Even the contention that practitioners learn through trial and error is untenable under these circumstances. Here practice is at the mercy of luck.

Although Shulman does not address these matters in any depth, his response to Sockett suggests an escape from the conundrum. Pursuing the golfing analogy, he writes:

> . . .top golfers try to anticipate, in a principled manner, the most likely difficulties they will encounter; they are both knowledgeable and skilled enough to *adapt to the unpredictable, precisely because it falls within highly predictable limits*. They have been champions because they possess the combination of knowledge, skill, motivation, and judgment needed to adapt *to the contingencies they encounter within the regularities they expect*. [my emphasis] (Shulman, 1987b, p. 475)

What are the "regularities" practitioners may expect with some certainty? In the case of golf "there is a predictable pattern to all golf courses" (Shulman, 1987b, p 475). Here lies a clue. There is a predictable pattern to all golf courses because of the rules that constitute the game. However unpredictable practices are, they are not random. In so far as the constitutive rules of a practice set limits to what will count as engagement in the practice, they provide a framework of expectation for practitioners. Sometimes the rules are explicitly recorded, as they are for games like golf and chess; at other times—especially with those central human practices like teaching and medicine—are implicit in the *telos* or overriding purpose of the practice.

There is another significant difference between games like golf and practices like teaching. The size, shape, and structure of the golf course are part of the constitutive rules of the game; whereas classrooms and schools are not constitutive of teaching. Teaching can take place almost anywhere; golf cannot be played without some semblance of a golf course. But perhaps this difference is unimportant for the point Shulman wants to make. Teacher education is centrally concerned with preparing them to work within the institutions that, in modern times, house, sustain, and control practice. While schools are not, strictly speaking, constitutive of teaching, they are the contexts in which practitioners are held accountable for their work.

Can wisdom-of-practice studies help us understand how excellent teachers acquire the judgment and skill required for adapting to contingencies they encounter within the regularities they expect? Sockett's criticisms suggest not. He accuses the wisdom-of-practice project of a myopic focus on content and of ignoring the difference that context and temperament make to excellent practice. I would argue that while particular researchers may do so (because of their limited situational appreciation, their failure to see and record nuance and detail), there is nothing in the idea of a study of wise practice that rules out proper attention to context, temperament, and other situational features. Indeed the attempt to characterize wise practice by looking at wise practitioners is consistent with an Aristotelian account of practical reasoning, or what Martha Nussbaum (1990) calls non-scientific deliberation.

On this account, neither the context of practice nor the temperament and character of the practitioner can be ignored or underplayed in judging the quality of a teacher's work. Sound practical judgment is defined by situational appreciation (Pendlebury, 1990; Wiggins, 1980). The teaching situation—which includes such things as the institutional context, the epistemic predicaments of the students, and the teacher's own talents and limitations—sets constraints on what is possible and constitutes the criteria for excellent practice. Sound practical judgment takes account both of what is ideal and of what is possible under particular circumstances.

Concluding Remarks

Neither the drive for efficiency nor the drive for effectiveness through research and measurement has succeeded in excluding luck from teaching. In different ways, they have succeeded in impoverishing the practice as well as its practitioners. To say this is not to say that efficiency and effectiveness have no place in excellent practice. Rather it is to claim that excellence in teaching cannot be reduced to the principles of efficient management or to a causal account of effectiveness. Nor, let me say in passing, can it be reduced to the procedure of simple weighing which is implied by instrumental accounts of practical reasoning in teaching.

Flawed as it may be, Shulman's attempt to spell out the nature and conditions of wise practice in teaching points to a more promising direction for an account of excellence. In teaching, excellence lies centrally in the marriage of what Aristotle calls practical and theoretical wisdom. Sockett's proposed criteria for an epistemology of practice may be seen as an attempt to sanction the marriage and to delineate the features which each of the two partners bring to it, and the extent and nature of their reciprocity. But it would be misleading to suppose that the marriage could exclude luck from practice. At best, it could bring about a rich understanding of the goods and ends of the practice and a realistic, clear-sighted perception of what is possible under different circumstances.

CHAPTER 3

Authority and the Tragic Dimension of Teaching

Nicholas C. Burbules

Authority, and what are legitimate grounds for authority, has long been one of the central moral issues surrounding teaching, even for those whose positions might otherwise have very little in common (for example, see Benne, 1986; Giroux, 1986; Haynes, 1986; Nash, 1966; Neiman, 1986; Nyberg and Farber, 1986; Peters, 1966; White, 1986). Because the role of a teacher requires asking questions, making requests, and providing information or advice that need to be trusted as reliable, the basis on which these activities can be performed legitimately, and why other participants in the teaching-learning process should cede some credibility to them, has been an ongoing concern for teachers at all levels of education.

From another vantage point, we need some demarcation of legitimate teacher authority, and the points at which it might be exceeded (by making arbitrary commands, by self-serving assertions of privilege, by holding forth on topics solely on the basis of one's own opinion and status, and so on); one cannot talk about whether teachers *abuse* their authority without having at least implicit assumptions about what the legitimate range of that authority ought to be.[1]

Unfortunately, for these purposes, the sorts of grounds on which teacher authority has been traditionally justified—knowledge, institutional status, age, and maturity, for example—have been thrown into doubt by various kinds of rebellion, intellectual and otherwise. On a more purely sociological level, the perceived authority of teachers has diminished as their public status has declined: Conservative parents do not want teachers exposing their children to ideas and values that do not conform with their own; poor and minority parents and students have in many cases abandoned the hope that education can provide significant opportunities to escape from the cycle of poverty and despair, and along with that loss of faith has come a loss of esteem for what teachers have to offer; and the increased bureaucratization and "deskilling" of teaching has robbed the occupation of much of the authority traditionally associated with the status of a "profession" (Burbules and Densmore, 1991a; 1991b).

On a more intellectual plane, scholars arguing from feminist and postmodern perspectives have challenged whether authority in *any* legitimate sense is appropriate to the teacher (Ellsworth, 1989; Nuyen, 1992). Drawing especially from the work of Michel Foucault (1980; 1988), postmodern critics have emphasized the power dynamics within which claims to knowledge, expertise, or institutionally-conferred status operate; since the social process by which these claims are made and legitimated tend to exclude and disadvantage subordinate groups, the claims to authority that rest upon them are suspect. They are regarded as forms of domination, albeit with a human face.

This essay attempts to take a fresh look at the problem of authority. It does seem, on the one hand, that for a teacher to organize and lead a classroom, to guide student learning, to evaluate student performance in some way (in other words, for a teacher to *teach*) does require some basis on which students will respect and, at least provisionally, cooperate in such activities. Yet it seems also true, on the other hand, that many of the traditional bases for asserting authority have been shaken by doubts about the certainty of knowledge, the justice of institutionally-conferred status and privileges, and the possibility of a completely impartial and benign exercise of authority solely "for the student's good." In the face of this tension, it seems to me, the very nature of authority and its relation to teaching need to be reconsidered. In this essay I will present a "tragic" characterization of teaching, and relate to that conception of teaching a view of authority that provides some normative basis for the activities that teachers need to perform in order to *be* teachers, without resting upon the unproblematized, foundationalist assumptions of knowledge and status that have been traditionally taken as the grounds of teacher authority.

Tragedy might seem at first to be an unusual characterization of teaching (Burbules, 1990; see also Arcilla, 1992). Teaching seems to be by nature a *hopeful* activity: the very endeavor of working intentionally to foster the learning and development of another requires an attitude of hopefulness and encouragement toward that possibility. Yet there is no paradox: this perspective of hope is itself part of the tragic sensibility. Unlike pessimism, which abandons hope, tragedy involves a dual perspective, one that recognizes possibilities as well as barriers, successes as well as failures, reasons for encouragement and reasons for doubt, without retreating into either naive utopianism or bitter cynicism (Burbules, 1986). The tragic sense acknowledges the real disappointments that life sometimes offers, and sees these as the *inevitable* byproducts of our very attempts at success; indeed, it sees the element of failure in every success, the loss in every gain. This profoundly ambivalent quality is strikingly true of teaching. Every student helped involves a student neglected; every new attainment comes at a cost; new understandings or realizations come at the price of losing some dearly-held memory, wish, or dream. And, to my way of thinking, this tragic element of teaching is not some unfortunate consequence of human failure or imperfectability—*it is a necessary feature of any kind of teaching worth its while.*

Teaching situations continually present teachers with alternative choices that cannot be pursued simultaneously. We cannot pursue all worthwhile lines of inquiry and we cannot help every student with every problem. Teaching requires us to make selections and establish priorities. These already difficult choices are exacerbated by problems such as limited time, swollen class sizes, and increasingly rigid legal and bureaucratic constraints, as well as factors that are almost completely beyond our influence, even as they impede and undermine our efforts—such as countereducational influences outside the school. This makes our range of discretion, in teaching as in many other human endeavors, a matter of making difficult choices among the options available to us, and often settling for imperfect but tolerable outcomes.

Furthermore, many of the goals that we do pursue entail mutually incompatible consequences. We can raise our academic expectations, but risk lowering the self-esteem of some students. We can emphasize the formation of valued character traits, but only at the expense of compromising a certain level of focus on academic excellence. We can become politically committed in our teaching efforts, but if so we run the risk of alienating a significant number of students (or their parents) whom we might otherwise influence. In fact, even our best-intentioned educational efforts have consequences that we can never know, since their effects show up long after our contact with students has passed. Sometimes, our very successes involve digging out the ground under our feet.

In light of these sorts of considerations, teaching should be seen as an inherently imperfect, uncertain, and incomplete process; and in every case there are parallel and equivalent kinds of imperfection, uncertainty, and incompleteness involved in the endeavor of learning. Thus a commitment to education means that one must place greater faith in the journey than in the certainty of reaching one's destination. What I have called the *tragic sense of education* involves an honest reflection on these limitations, without abandoning the educational effort entirely: this doubled perspective requires us "to undermine our hope with doubt, and to fight against our skepticism with persistent effort for the better" (Burbules, 1990, p. 472).

The tragic perspective does not, in any sense, mean that we should abandon the attempt to teach and learn with others. But it does prepare us for the difficult and uncertain tradeoffs that attempt requires of us; it leads us to a more modest and honest admission of the limits on what teaching can achieve; and it encourages us to recognize the interdependence we have with our students (and other educationally significant role-players, particularly parents), whom we should come to see as our partners in striving to attain realistic and sustainable goals, not as beneficiaries of our paternalistic vision of what will be good for them. If we, as teachers, become a bit less certain and confident, it might help us in forging a closer respect and reciprocity with our students and their parents. This, in turn, might open up some avenues for responding to the sociological challenges to teacher authority discussed earlier.

As I have said, the larger vision of teaching and learning that develops from this understanding is one that stresses *process* rather than *outcome*. Like Sisyphus, we need to focus our educational efforts on the moment, the opportunities present at hand, and focus less teleologically on an anticipated set of outcomes (Camus, 1969). Too often in schooling, and perhaps more frequently now, when the evaluation of students, teachers, and indeed entire school systems, is being tied so closely to quantitative outcome measures, the quality of the teaching relation and the openness of both teachers and students to spontaneous occasions for discovery and exploration are being sacrificed for the sake of outcomes-based learning objectives (Benne, 1986).

This criticism is not meant to suggest that the having of goals, some relatively specific or proximate, others more general or long term, is unsuitable for teaching; in some sense such goals are inherent in all human action. But an excessive reliance on these can make teachers and students overly preoccupied on the "payoff" of their activities, and too little concerned with the quality of the relation that joins them, and with the spirit of serendipity that ought to accompany all authentic teaching-learning opportunities. If we cannot be too certain about the efficacy and outcomes of our educational relations and activities, at least we can have some confidence in the value of these relations and activities themselves. This means that how we express such traits of character as the virtues of open-mindedness, curiosity, concern, and respect for ourselves and for others in those relations and activities becomes more of an educational touchstone than our search for higher test scores or check-offs on some list of behavioral outcomes. We should strive to create a pedagogical relation of mutual commitment, respect, and inquiry with our students, not because it is certain to succeed in the attainment of learning outcomes, but because we value the quality of that relation, despite its uncertainty of success. If we are to fail, then, at least it will be in the context of educational relations and activities that are authentic and humane.

Growing out of these considerations, it should be clear, will be a changing conception of teacher authority. Many traditional justifications for authority rest on teleological assumptions: that teachers know what students need to learn; that their role is to lead students into the beliefs, values, and dispositions of "adulthood" and "mature understandings"; that learning is directed toward participation in the workplace and the community and that educators (or parents) know best what the outlines of that participation ought to be for each student. And, as Elizabeth Ellsworth (1989) has rightly noted, such presumptions are not limited to conservative or reactionary views of education, but to many ostensibly "liberal" or "progressive" views as well. It does seem that where questions of teacher authority are concerned, teleological and paternalistic (or maternalistic) postures are extremely difficult to avoid.

Here, I would like to develop in more detail what the *tragic* vision of teaching might entail for questions of teacher authority, and to suggest how embracing the contradictions and uncertainties inherent in the teaching role can help to make us more modest, more sensitive, and thereby potentially more "effective" as teachers.

The central element in this revision of the teacher role is an abandonment of what Dewey (1929) called the "quest for certainty," an expectation of final answers, unproblematic consensus, and resolvable dilemmas. The quest for certainty underlies what I have been calling a teleological conception of teacher authority; the belief that teacher authority is justified by the ends it produces. This kind of authority ultimately rests upon the foundation or "knowledge base" sought by a great deal of educational research intended to "professionalize" teaching. Authority grounded in expertise or experience, for example, makes sense only because of the implicit assumption that expertise and experience are likely to yield certain educational ends by means of putative laws, principles, or rules. This is not to say that expertise and experience are irrelevant to legitimate teacher authority; but that the typical reasons for valuing them presume a confidence about specific outcomes that—if my earlier comments are correct—cannot honestly be sustained by a mature and reflective teacher.

But the problem with a teleological justification for teacher authority rests with the fact that the outcomes guaranteed by "professional" expertise and experience are more uncertain than can be promised. A separate problem is that the learning outcomes highlighted by this sense of authority, even when they might be achieved, are not the only effects teaching has. When it highlights goals that are epistemic (such as learning subject matter) and narrow (assessable by standardized tests), the teleological conception of authority risks ignoring the "hidden curriculum" of learning outcomes that have more to do with learning roles of subordination in hierarchical institutional contexts; internalizing implicit lessons about dependency on authoritative sources of knowledge; and overlooking silences or gaps which inevitably exist, given the limits on what any teacher can offer, but which communicate definite, if inadvertent, messages to students about what the school considers worth knowing. The potential consequences of this latent teaching and learning process are to develop an exaggerated faith in the truths one learns from the authoritative teacher and a corresponding denigration of alternative beliefs and values, often including one's own or those of one's cultural group. These latent effects are also "outcomes" of teaching; yet the teleological conception of authority, with its emphasis on teacher expertise and experience, tends to obscure, not illuminate them.

The justification of teacher authority in terms of institutional role or professional status are, less obviously, teleological justifications as well. The legitimacy of such justifications, first of all, has been questioned by many feminist authors as compatible with the spirit of egalitarian teaching and learning. Ellsworth (1989), for example, levels some sharp criticisms against the attempt to legitimate the special role and status of teachers in contexts of higher education. The presentation and protection of such forms of institutionally-conferred authority serve a purpose beyond the benefit of students: namely, the perpetuation of certain roles and privileges that are to the *teacher's* benefit. These are frequently justified by saying that, even when they are abused, or when they might not immediately serve students' interests, they are nevertheless beneficial, "overall and in the long run." This is a risky sort of justification for any educational relation or activity, since it frequently puts us in the position of sacrificing present values for the sake of purported future benefits—benefits about which we must be quite skeptical in many concrete cases.

And Ellsworth identifies a crucial issue: that personal authority in a teaching situation cannot be abstracted from the institutional history and social context that arrogate to the teacher privileges and status to which she or he may not be entitled. The teacher may not desire these, but they are not avoided simply by saying one does not choose or intend them. To this she responds, speaking of herself: "A preferable goal seemed to be to become capable of a sustained encounter with currently oppressive formations and power relations...and to enter into the encounter in a way that owned up to my own implications in those formations and was capable of changing my own relation to and investments in those formations" (Ellsworth, 1989, p. 308). Because there are many institutional influences that arrogate to teachers a status and privileges that exceed—and in fact interfere with—the formation of an authority relation that can be defended, such factors often need to be brought under critical scrutiny *within* the teaching-learning relation. Rather than trying to ignore such constraints, I believe that Ellsworth is correct that a more honest stance is to own up to this situation and encourage students to question it, rather than pretending that because one has good intentions one is somehow shielded from criticism. Certainly, the *presumption* of authority, and the privileges and status that go with it, should be avoided. Taking such privileges and status for granted yields *authoritarianism*, which has no place in educational settings.

Yet I do not see how we avoid some sort of authority in every educational endeavor, no matter how earnestly we strive for egalitarian pedagogical relations. Nor is authority necessarily a threat to such egalitarian relations. We are continually in situations where we seek to gain information from a better-informed source, advice from an experienced mentor, insight from a friend who knows us well, direction from a group facilitator, and so on. These are all instances of authority. While it is essential that credible authority not be taken for granted, but be periodically scrutinized and re-established, this scrutiny cannot take place continuously, and at particular moments such authority will be an unstated element in an ongoing teaching and learning relation. The question ought to be framed, then: What *types* of educational authority are justified? Here, the tragic perspective on teaching helps to inform our understanding.

The justification of authority in terms of institutional role reifies what are in many cases problematic positions of status and privilege; and justifications of authority in terms of expertise and experience are often simply thinly-veiled pleas back to institutional status, such as graduate degrees. Justifications in terms of expertise and experience also run the risk of taking for granted conceptions of knowledge that depend upon presuppositions of objectivity and universality that deny the diversity we encounter in most teaching situations—a diversity within which many rightly regard the authoritative teacher as a potentially unilateral and peremptory foreclosure on alternative possibilities. Finally, justifications of teacher authority in terms of expertise and experience focus on the qualities of the individual teacher as the criteria of legitimate authority, rather than on the quality of the teaching and learning *relation* which can be forged by a teacher and student together, and which can evolve over time. As I have suggested, it is a far better approach to work at creating the most educationally supportive relation between teacher and student for *present* purposes, and to trust that such a relation, properly established and sustained, will have the capacity to develop into forms appropriate at each stage for the type of teaching and learning opportunities that are suited for each partner. In such a relation, to be sure, teacher knowledge, experience, and expertise will play important roles; but they are not themselves the grounds of teacher authority. Rather, authority becomes a *relational* concept, arising from the particular bonds of respect, concern, and trust that particular teachers and students establish among themselves. Authority in this sense exists neither before nor beyond the interactions, communicative and otherwise, that join two or more parties in a relation of mutuality and shared interest.

Thinking of teaching and learning as a relation, and as an inherently imperfect and incomplete process, helps to address several of the aforementioned problems of teacher authority. First, a relational attitude toward teaching involves asking seriously the questions "Who am I?" and "With whom am I interacting?" On one hand, it is not enough to frame one's position in terms of a particular role ("I'm a teacher") or to justify one's authority simply by reference to that role. In many ways, as discussed, this risks arrogating to oneself privileges and status one may not deserve. At the same time, one must be honest with oneself about the knowledge, insights, or talents one does possess, and which led one to the educational situation in the first place. It is also important to be open about the satisfactions one derives from playing a role in others' learning—after all, why else do we become teachers?

On the other hand, it is important to understand the perspective of one's partners in the teaching and learning situation: What motivates them to enter into the process? What do they stand to learn and what do they stand to teach us? What tendencies might they have to defer to us whether we desire it or not? What experiences or contextual factors might interfere with their ability or willingness to enter into a fully mutual communicative partnership with us? Moreover, it is not enough simply to reflect on such factors introspectively: they often need to be raised explicitly and discussed as aspects of the relation at hand. In many educational contexts, the critical examination of authority can further the process of re-examining educational aims and methods; yet it seems equally clear that a consensual authority, a respectful deferral to the experience or expertise of one's partner, might well emerge from such discussions. I see no reason to assume that it cannot, or should not. (But this is a *nonteleological* justification.)

Second, the nature of any teaching and learning relation over time is that it is fluid: roles shift back and forth; patterns of interaction change; various reversals might take place. In an ongoing relation, clear demarcations between teaching moments and learning moments are impossible. Even if one person is doing all the questioning and the other all the answering (to pick an extreme case), both parties still stand to learn. Furthermore, topics within the teaching and learning encounter change, and this change might mean that a partner more knowledgeable in one area may stand to learn from the other in a different area. This sort of shifting pattern does not mean that there is no authority, but simply that authority cannot be singularly attached to one participant.

Third, listening is an important aspect of legitimate authority, not only as a way in which one stands to learn something new, but also as a concrete relational activity that alters the status of one's authority (Burbules and Rice, 1991; 1992; Rice and Burbules, 1993). Listening exhibits respect, interest, and concern for one's partner. It is a specific way of enabling another's voice to be heard. It is an active process, not just a passive receptivity, and can itself encourage others to develop and express their own independent point of view. Beyond listening, an effective authority relation also requires sensitivity to the environmental circumstances, institutional contexts, personal histories, or interpersonal dynamics that impede participation in an educational activity. It often will not be enough just to listen; one might have to work actively to create an environment in which a silenced voice feels the confidence or security to speak.

Fourth, authority within a teaching and learning relation must be to some degree self-undermining over time. There may be cases in which a particular claim to authority must be taken at face value, because to demand a complete justification of that claim would distract necessary time and attention from a problem at hand. But the aim of teaching should be to make such cases less frequent over time; to create a situation in which authority as a basis for certain communicative privileges is no longer appropriate—in which, conceivably, one's partners come to the point where they reject one's authority or find it no longer necessary for their development. To my way of thinking, an authority that is not open to this possibility does run the risk of taking its own status too seriously. Yet at the same time I would say that a teacher who *can* offer perspectives and insights that would foster the development and autonomy of a partner, but refuses to do so because of a misguided or disingenuous rejection of authority in any form, does the other no good service.

Of course, even such choices as encouraging the questioning of one's authority, or provisionally setting it aside, are decisions that only a person in authority has the latitude to make; indeed, such decisions have the effect they do, in many cases, precisely because it is clear in all parties' minds that they occur within a broader framework in which authority is agreed to. It seems that the very notion of being a teacher entails the claim to some degree of legitimate authority; all the interesting questions arise in examining what justifies that authority, how it can best be exercised for educational purposes, and what limits it should be bounded by. Of course, some problematic assertions of authority will still exist, and the danger is that participants will slip back into institutionally-reinforced patterns from time to time; there are, for many of us, attractions to being held as an authority, or in deferring to others as such. But even where such mistakes will be made, students of all ages can be quite resilient and creative in finding ways to deflect unwarranted authority. To assume a devastating and oppressive impact in every problematic assertion of authority is (ironically) to exaggerate the power teachers have in many situations; while we should certainly criticize problematic assertions of authority and avoid them ourselves to the degree that we can, at the same time we should not underestimate students by assuming that what we claim is necessarily what they grant us.[2]

Thus, authority in the context of a teaching and learning relation can have legitimacy, based neither in institutionalized roles and privileges nor in unexamined assumptions about knowledge and professional expertise. Rather, authority can be seen as growing out of an ongoing communicative interchange that acknowledges differences in knowledge, experience, or ability without reifying them; that allows for changing authority relations over time or from topic to topic; that manifests reciprocity and respect by who listens as well as by who speaks; and that can evolve toward a relation in which authority no longer need be a necessary or appropriate status for *either* participant (Burbules, 1993). Admittedly, our fulfillment of these intentions will be imperfect—as mentioned, an important barrier to this effort will be institutional and historical definitions of an authority role that persist even when participants resist them. The tragic perspective on teacher authority prepares us for the precarious balance we need to maintain between provisionally accepting certain roles within an ongoing relation, in large part for the very purpose of rendering those roles superfluous at some later time; and it prepares us for the inevitable fact that we will, on occasion, lose ourselves in these roles, arrogating to ourselves (or to our partners) a presumed and privileged authority that is not justified by the relation. Acknowledging this fact in advance is one of the factors that helps establish a context in which it is *possible* to disclose and criticize this eventuality, when it occurs. Imagining that expertise, experience, or good will somehow assure only a benevolent teacher authority rests, unfortunately, on a fond illusion—precisely the type of illusion that critically-minded teachers should be trying to overcome, in themselves as well as their students.

This conception of teacher authority attempts to respond sympathetically to the feminist and postmodern criticisms discussed earlier. It does not rest on authoritative views of knowledge, truth, or expertise; on unproblematized assumptions of power or position relative to others; on reified ideas about who is the "teacher" and who is the "learner" in educational settings; or on decontextual and universalistic assumptions about what a person held in "authority" can say and do, apart from the particular relations in which that person is joined to others. Although it is beyond the scope of this essay, I would suggest that the view I am presenting situates authority within an ongoing communicative relation of negotiation and reciprocity: a relation in which authority might be provisionally ceded, but in which it is continually open to scrutiny, questioning, and challenge (Burbules, 1993; see also Haynes, 1986). Authority in this sense is a "bootstrapped" relation, established in terms that do not take for granted any conditions that cannot be presented and justified, at some level, in the context of the relation at hand (Neiman, 1986). Over time, this type of authority will change, and eventually recede—especially in educational settings, where the very point to the teaching-learning relation is directed toward making authority superfluous, as I have said.

In conclusion, a teaching and learning relation should be aimed toward making authority superfluous; but teacher authority, properly conceived and sensitively exercised, can be a helpful element in attaining that end. For example, dialogue as a pedagogical relation constitutes in form and process a practical *repudiation* of hierarchical conceptions of authority: it exemplifies the core values of mutual respect, egalitarianism, open participation, and reciprocity in the teaching-learning relation—perhaps more so than any other sort of pedagogical relation (see Freire 1970). As Michael Oakeshott (1962, p. 198) says, "voices that speak in connection do not compose a hierarchy."

Authority should be seen as constituted within an ongoing teaching and learning relation, neither preceding nor transcending it. The authority anyone deserves to have is one that can be credibly established and maintained in terms that others grant credence to; an authority that cannot withstand such scrutiny is an authority not worth having.

CHAPTER 4

Style and the Art of Teaching

_____ *James W. Garrison*

Near the end of the title chapter of his book *The Aims of Education* A. N. Whitehead (1929; 1967) stated, "Style...is the last acquirement of the educated mind; it is also the most useful. It pervades the whole being...the artisan with a sense for style prefers good work. Style is the ultimate morality of mind" (p. 12). For Whitehead style was as much an intellectual and aesthetic as it was a moral virtue. Indeed style was the ultimate morality because it so intimately involved the other two virtues. I believe Whitehead was right that a sense of *individual* style should be among the most important aims of teacher preparation.

The second wave of educational reform stresses the role of teacher empowerment, teacher leadership, and teacher professionalism in school decision making and the restructuring of education. Ironically, although not surprisingly, the intellectual, aesthetic, and moral virtue of individual style has been entirely omitted from papers and reports that talk about teacher leadership and professionalism. The need for teachers to develop their own individual and unique style is a gap in the contemporary educational conversation concerning teacher empowerment.

Whitehead (1929; 1967) saw style as "an aesthetic sense, based on admiration for the direct attainment of a foreseen end, simply and without waste" (p. 12). For Whitehead "above style, and above knowledge, there is something, a vague shape like fate above the Greek gods. That something is power. Style is the fashioning of power, the restraining of power...the power of attainment of the desired end is fundamental" (p. 12). I do not want to enter into a debate here as to the nature of power. Considering power in terms of its ability to secure desired ends should be insightful, even if it does not exhaust the meaning of the word. Style, on Whitehead's account, is the economic fashioning of power for a purpose, and he defines it as an efficiency of a kind that the utilitarian accountant cannot comprehend. Whitehead (1929; 1967) wrote:

. . .with style the end is attained without issue, without raising undesirable inflammations. With style you attain your end and nothing but your end. With style the effect of your activity is calculable, and foresight is the last gift of gods to men (sic). With style your power is increased, for your mind is not distracted with irrelevancies, and you are more likely to attain you object. Now style is the exclusive privilege of the expert. (pp. 12–13)

Again, I think that Whitehead is correct. To talk of teacher empowerment, professionalism, and leadership without talking about individual style is misguided.

In what follows we will see how certain disciplinary technologies and attitudes toward science are used *on* teachers to control them. It will be shown that this control eliminates the component of style in classroom teaching thereby creating a gap in the conversation about educational reform. In the conclusion I will suggest that without individual style in teaching it is impossible for teaching or its reform to be creative and intelligent. The result will be shown to be undemocratic.

Disciplinary Technology and the Art of Teaching

It has been well documented that schools in the United States are organized in accordance with the principles of scientific management and technocratic efficiency. These organizational theories stress external control and manipulation. Professional autonomy and judgement are eliminated by means of techniques that require conformity to "hyperationalized" policy mandates, standardized practices, and reductive notions of accountability that submits both teachers and students to the assault of a battery of examinations that document their performance (see Callahan, 1962; Wise 1979; 1988; Wirth, 1983; 1992). Management By Objectives (MBO) has dominated organizational theory in the United States for over thirty years. The idea in government is to give the taxpayer "the most bang for the buck" by maximizing the productivity function. This is achieved by minimizing inputs like human capital and maximizing outputs. In Vietnam, the output measure was "the body count," in education it has been the SAT. Perhaps the most sinister portrayal of this sad situation is provided by Michel Foucault (1979) in his *Discipline and Punish*. In particular, I have in mind his discussion of the "technology of power" and how well it fits education in the Western democracies (see McKinney and Garrison, 1993).

Foucault (1979) presents us with "a history of the utilitarian rationalization of detail in moral accountability and political control" (p. 139). This version of utilitarian thinking is in the same line that gave us "cost-benefit analysis"; a version of the utilitarian calculator for modern liberal democracies. In a "hyperrationalized" technocracy morality and good performance are determined by conformity to bureaucratic rules as determined by technical instruments of evaluation. Foucault (1979) describes three instruments of disciplinary power. They are "hierarchical observation, normalizing judgement, and their combination in a procedure that is specific to it, examination" (p. 170). To understand hierarchical observation just think about the functioning of the typical school intercom system; or the relations between teachers, principals, the central office, superintendent, and schoolboard. The observational hierarchy is really a circle expressing relations of power, control, and domination.

Another important part of the technology of power is "normalizing judgment." In normalizing judgment "all behavior falls in the field between good and bad marks, good and bad points. Moreover, it is possible to quantify this field and work out an arithmetical economy based on it. A penal accountancy, constantly brought up to date, makes it possible to obtain the punitive balance-sheet of each individual" (Foucault, 1979, p. 180). Normalizing judgment puts a cruel twist on modernity's glorification of the autonomous individual. Finally, Foucault (1979) found that "the examination is at the centre of the procedures that constitute the individual as effect and object of power, as effect and object of knowledge. It is the examination which, by confining hierarchical surveillance and normalizing judgment, assures the great disciplinary functions of distribution and classification...and combinatory individuality" (p. 192). The disciplinary tool of examination is the cash for the economy of accountability that technocratic liberal instrumentalism cannot do without. Every reform of education seriously proposed in the last three decades has relied on measurable outcomes as the linchpin.

Foucault (1983) himself thought each individual immersed in webs of power/knowledge and so proclaimed, "My problem is not that everything is bad, but that everything is dangerous. . . . If everything is dangerous, then we always have something to do. So my position leads not to apathy but to a hyper and pessimistic activism. I think that the ethical and political choice we have to make every day is to determine which is the main danger" (1983, pp. 231–232). Foucault's (1984) solution to the problem is "maturity."

Hubert Dreyfus and Paul Rabinow (1986) attempt to explicate what Foucault meant by "maturity": "Maturity consists in not only a *heroic* but what Foucault calls an ironic stance toward one's present situation" (p. 113). The heroic views life as a continuous struggle to be free. It is an aesthetic of dramatic action. The meaning is in what is created along the way. Aestheticism replaces morality as following pre-established rules and norms. Foucault himself wrote:

> ...the problem is to free oneself...one has to dig out of a whole mass of discourse that has accumulated...when it is a matter of determining the system of discourse in which we are still living, when we have to question the words that are still echoing in our ears, which became confused with those we are trying to formulate, the archaeologist, like the Nietzschian philosopher, is forced to take a hammer to it." (cited in Sheridan, 1980, p. 196)

We will be especially concerned with what technocratic discourse does to individual style. Foucault here does not seem to realize that the practice of *ars politica* requires the artistic sensitivity of the tuning hammer as much as the sledge hammer. Dreyfus and Rabinow (1986) define the ironic as "an abandonment of traditional seriousness while preserving active engagement in the concerns of the present" and "in seeking in the present those practices which offer the possibility of a new way of acting" (p. 117). This is the mature sense of irony described by Alven Neiman in chapter 5. They note that Foucault associated the ironic ideal with poetry, and especially the poet of Baudelaire. Foucault (1984) himself affirmed, "the asceticism of the dandy who makes of his body, his behavior, his feelings, and passions his very existence, a work of art. Modern man, for Baudelaire, is not the man who goes off to discover himself, his secrets, and his hidden truth; he is the man who tries to invent himself. This modernity does not "liberate man (sic) in his being"; "it compels him to face the task of producing himself" (pp. 41–42). Foucault goes on to affirm that "ironic heroization" does not "have any place in society itself, or in the body politic;" it "can only be produced in another, a different place, which Baudelaire calls art" (p. 42). This is the dualism that separates Foucault from Dewey, as well as from teachers and teaching.

When asked who opposes whom in the politics of struggle within relationships of power/knowledge, Foucault (1980) responded, "I would say it's all against all....We all fight against each other" (p. 208). This is the kind of silly and destructive irony described by Neiman. In the end, Foucault, the postmodernist, falls for one of modernity's most debilitating dogmas; that is, the belief in the autonomous, even if arational, self. I applaud the postmodern notion of maturity as more important than morality viewed as mere rule following and obedience to power elites who invoke the knowledge of science to establish their rules. However, I prefer the more social and communicative sense of tragedy and irony described elsewhere in the present volume by Nicholas Burbules and Alven Neiman (see chapters 3 and 5). As a teacher, I personally cannot accept the ideal of the dandy if it means a "self which can nevertheless survive the pursuit of happiness to be found in someone else...." Nor, do I believe, will any competent practitioner of the teaching profession. There is ample evidence to support this opinion.

Dan Lortie's *Schoolteacher: A Sociological Study* (1975) remains the most complete report on the social world of the classroom teacher. Lortie found that of the more than 5,800 teachers surveyed over 76.5% said that for them the primary rewards of teaching were what Lortie called the "psychic" rewards. Only 11.9% chose extrinsic rewards like salary and status, and only 11.7% choose ancillary rewards like summers off (Lortie, 1975, p. 105). By psychic rewards teachers meant such things as "knowing that I have reached students and they have learned," and a "chance to associate with other teachers." Another psychic reward not included in this particular survey, but discussed throughout Lortie's report, is the exercise of creative autonomy in the classroom. This particular psychic reward led to the most conflict with administration and other agencies outside the classroom. McCloskey, Provenzo, Cohn, and Kottkamp (1991) found almost the same identical results when they replicated Lortie's study in the same Florida school district (see especially p. 254). What I would like to call attention to is the fact that when teachers heroically seek self-creation and creative self-expression they think of it in terms of their relations to others, and especially their students (see Lortie, 1975, p. 28). That is just part of what it means to be a competent practitioner in a caring profession.

Teachers seek creative autonomy not selfishly for themselves, but in order to achieve their special ends, "knowing that I have reached students and they have learned." The twenty-first of the twenty-eight definitions of "style" offered by *Oxford English Dictionary* (1971) reads, "A particular mode or form of skilled construction, execution or production; the manner in which a work of art is executed regarded as characteristic of the individual artist or of his time and place; one of the modes recognized in a particular art as suitable for the production of beautiful or skillful work." To paraphrase Whitehead, with style teachers can calculate and foresee the effect of their activity. With style their power is increased. Style is always the privilege of the expert, the professional. For teachers, when they know that they have reached students, and the students have learned, the good and the beautiful converge. It is a convergence that, to achieve with any regularity, calls for a great deal of professional knowledge and its intelligent application in practice.

Richard Rorty (1982) believes that "we should see Dewey as having already gone the route Foucault is traveling, and as having arrived at the point Foucault is still trying to reach.... Foucault does not, as far as I can see, do more than update Dewey by warning that the social scientists have often been, and are always likely to be co-opted by the bad guys" (p. 207). Many readers of Dewey ignore his many discussions of "social control" such as we find especially in the opening chapters of *Democracy And Education*. The difference between Foucault and Dewey on Rorty's (1982) account is that Dewey "allows room for unjustifiable hope, and an ungroundable but vital sense of human solidarity" (p. 208). Although Dewey surely offers no metaphysical or epistemological foundation, I believe that he gives us a justifiable hope and a vital sense of democratic solidarity. In this paper I will try to show how well Dewey over seventy years ago understood the kind of thinking that leads to the establishment of disciplinary technologies in teaching, and how democratic social relations can overcome them without abandoning the benefits better technology might offer.

The Scientific Temper and the Scientific Technique

Because the results of educational research are so often used on them as instruments of control, and even domination, teachers often view scientific knowledge as threatening, a tool of social oppression and artistic alienation that suppresses their specialized practical knowledge. Teachers are often, therefore, hostile toward educational research that they see as irrelevant even as they are required to conform to the rules and policy that it underwrites. The result is one version of the conflict between scientific theory on one side and the personal morality and desire for creative self expression characteristic of practice on the other. Rather than construct some bridge across the gap let us close it by following Dewey, and Bertrand Russell, in drawing a distinction that dissolves this false dualism.

In his book *Religion and Science*, Russell distinguishes between two different attitudes toward science. They are the "scientific temper" and the "scientific technique" (Russell, 1935; 1968, pp. 245–246). Russell found the former attitude the healthier for it is "cautious, tentative, and piecemeal; it does not imagine that it knows the whole truth, or even at its best knowledge is wholly true. It knows that every doctrine needs emendation sooner or later, and that the necessary emendation requires freedom of investigation and freedom of discussion" (cited in Dewey, 1946, p. 172). The scientific technique has the status of a secular religion in which the scientific experts and technocrats serve as the high priests. Russell wrote, "The practical experts who employ scientific technique and still more the government and large firms [and school districts] which employ the practical experts, acquire a quite different temper from that of men [and woman] of science—a temper full of a sense of limitless power, of arrogant certainty, and of pleasure in manipulation of even human material" (cited in Dewey, 1946, p. 148). The scientific technique is concerned not with the process of scientific inquiry, but exclusively with the certain truths it is perceived to produce. Similarly, the products of science are assumed to be means that are useful instruments for achieving any end.

John Dewey, who certainly had his disagreements with Russell, nonetheless embraces Russell's distinction wholeheartedly. Nor is it hard to see why. According to Dewey, all thinking was a continuous and never-ending process of inquiry whose purpose was to solve practical problems like how to help people learn. That is to say that for Dewey all inquiry is an exercise in means-ends reasoning. Although it is possible in imagination to separate the process (means) from the product (ends), in actual practice it is never wise to do so. We will explore this bit of practical wisdom more extensively later.

For present purposes, it is sufficient to note that for Dewey the major shortcoming of the scientific technique is that it separates means from ends, the process from the product. Dewey (1946) wrote:

"Science...is still something that a group of persons, called scientists, do; something they do in laboratories, observatories, and places of special research [and surely not classrooms]... The prestige of science is due for the most part not to general adoption of its temper of mind but to its material application....the material power...." (pp. 173–174)

The intellectually, artistically, and morally liberating process of inquiry is still something participated in by only a small group of persons called scientists, while all the rest of humankind seems fated, or content, to distribute or consume its material products and power. Wise's "legislated learning" and Foucault's "disciplinary technology" document the reign of "practical experts" who use the products of inquiry merely to manage "human material." Scientific technique converts the products of scientific inquiry into instruments of external control and distorted social relations that empower a few and oppress many.

Scientific Technique and
Teacher "Performance Measurement"

Scientific technique can, perhaps, dictate artistic performance, but it cannot command a quality aesthetic performance. The results are often as uninspiring and undesirable as the technically correct yet hollow and mechanical player piano. Keith L. Raitz (1989) attributes such unsatisfying, unaesthetic, and inhuman performances to what he calls "detached technique." Technique, Raitz (1989) tells us, is "instrumental" to some goal or purpose and "as a practical matter, technique has no value except in relation to ends" (p. 53). What makes technique intelligent and rational is the end, purpose, or value for which it is employed. Even the best musicians practice their scales to reinforce certain habits of good performance that, since they can be carried out effortlessly, releases them to attend to the more difficult, refined, and creative aspects of their performance. Detached technique, by contrast, assumes that it can detach behaviors from the purposes that give them meaning and value and transform them into mere means to indeterminate ends. Detached techniques are generic and value neutral, or so it is claimed, because they have been disconnected from any particular human goal, purpose, or value.

Raitz develops a critique of process-product research of teaching and its implementation by the Florida Performance Measurement System (FPMS), a teacher performance measurement system that became the model for similar systems that were eventually implemented by most states in the union. The FPMS was an outcomes assessment teacher evaluation system that was so unsuccessful that many states, like my home state of Virginia, soon abandoned it. Still the "scientific technique" that went into the design and implementation of first-wave behaviorally driven FPMS remains and is coming back in the second wave of the 1990s as cognitive judgment and practical reasoning in teacher assessment. Its application to students is, of course, passed on to the teachers that must teach to the tests that all such programs require to measure "performance."

Raitz's critique is inspired by Kurt Vonnegut's novel *Player Piano*. This novel is set in Ilium, New York sometime in the finely tuned technocratic, rather than democratic, future of the United States. Ilium has successfully used Tayloristic time-motion studies and expert systems analysis to abstract techniques from the finest practitioners. In this novel, men operating metal lathes is the paradigm. The operator's techniques were studied and automated eventually putting the lath operators out of work. Expert systems analysis created a two-tiered social system in Ilium. On the upper layer of the hierarchy, and living on one side of the river in Ilium, are the scientists, technicians, and technocratic administrators. Below and on the other side of the river are the "Reeks and Wrecks," the service people and unskilled laborers. This situation is of course a real future possibility (see, for example, Wirth, 1992).

Raitz sees process-product and most other research *on* teachers, as well as its use, again on them, by state technocrats, as leading to a situation similar to what happened to the lath operators in Ilium. The teachers, however, will retain their jobs, but their performance will be monitored by FPMS. Raitz (1989) writes:

> ...the Florida Performance Measurement System....claimed by its authors to be the state of the art in teacher effectiveness, identifies 121 "specific teacher behaviors that have been shown through research to be directly related to increased student achievement and improved classroom conduct," behaviors that "are generic across patterns of teaching and do not prescribe a particular teaching style or mode of instruction."...What is being claimed by the authors of the Florida System is that there exists a set of effective techniques that are in a certain sense neutral. Supposedly, these techniques have been observed by researchers in the behavior of effective teachers exhibiting a wide variety of teaching styles. (p. 51)

What both the twenty-first definition of style in the *Oxford English Dictionary* (1971) and Whitehead's statements regarding style have in common is the particular way that the individual artists achieves their individual ends and carries out their unique construction. Whitehead, for his part, thinks that there is also a moral dimension to style. However, the state bureaucrats in Florida, and the dozens of states that followed their lead, did not think that the 121 "specific teacher behaviors" interfered with an individual teacher's style even as they applied an external measurement system that reductively evaluated good teaching performance exclusively in terms of those behaviors. The Florida Performance Measurement System entirely ignored the aesthetic and moral dimensions of teaching. It was assumed that those could be detached from the artist's repertoire of behaviors necessary for the intelligent practice of teaching. Perhaps the mildest thing we might say about these technocrats is that they are truly modern in their acceptance of a sharp separation between the theoretical or "science" from the practical, i.e., aesthetics and ethics. A bit more critically we might note their willingness to use the knowledge of educational research on even "human material" as part of a Foucaultian disciplinary technology.

In Raitz's opinion, all 121 behaviors are detached techniques. They are detached both from the specific individual purposes of the teachers, or even parents and schools, as well as the intellectual, aesthetic, and moral context that gives them meaning. They are very similar to what Burbules called "detached principles." The claim of the FPMS is that these behaviors are generic; yet as Raitz notes, if we are to interpret these mechanical behaviors as meaningful, we must attribute individual human purposes to them. Raitz's (1989) example is instructive:

> Consider the technique of "eye contact," described in *Domains* as follows: "teacher looks at students steadily and intensely without glaring, suspiciousness, or anger." Eye contact, for a Socratic teacher, is peering through the windows of some pupil's soul; for a Deweyan teacher, it is trying to gauge the breadth and depth of some child's experience; for a Florida System teacher, it is trying to control some student's behavior, keep the student on task, and so on. Thus, eye contact is a full-bodied technique of the Florida System, as are the other 120 that are listed. They are not generic. (p. 57)

What we have here is "luck diminishment" run amuck. Raitz seems to want to conclude that there are no generic teaching techniques because there are no detached techniques.

Raitz, however, seems to go a bit too far. In his response to Raitz, Gary D. Fenstermacher defends "general methods." Fenstermacher (1989) argues that it is acceptable to "separate means and ends, to detach teaching technique from the reasons and purposes for teaching" (p. 63). "Such detachment is evident," Fenstermacher (1989) finds, "in the novice piano player practicing chords...." (p. 64). Fenstermacher (1989) concludes:

> The problem arises when the technique stays detached, and forms the essential character of the enterprise to be under-taken....This forming of the detached technique into the constitutive rule of teaching is what the Florida Performance Measurement System has done to knowledge gained from process-product research. It is not the research itself that is culprit, as Raitz argues. It is district, state, and federal mandates

that turn the findings of the research into what amount to definitions of effective teaching. (p. 65)

It is hard not to agree with Fenstermacher. Teachers had no part in the production of the knowledge that will be used on them, that the state will mandate ends as well as means in the form of standards of learning, e.g., "literacy passports" and all will be sewn together by a system of tests, the acme of Foucault's disciplinary technology. Style is destroyed in such circumstances.

So what is lost when the state destroys individual style by mandating means and ends, and enforcing the mandates by employing a disciplinary technology? The straightforward answer is creative autonomy along with the other psychic rewards of teaching. The result is frustration, fatigue, stress, depression, and the other symptoms of teacher burnout. A somewhat more sophisticated analysis of the same thing is Marx's analysis of "Alienated Labor" (see Bottomore, 1963, pp. 120 ff.). Alienation on Marx's analysis is artistic in character and has four unfortunate effects. First, the artist is alienated from the artifact. Their creative energies are put into ends that are alien to them since they had no say in the deliberations that determined them. Worse still, the artist's very individual behavioral acts, that are turned into means for achieving the ends of someone else, are then standardized to measure the artist's performance. Second, because human beings are fundamentally creative and productive beings, alienation from the product of one's own creative energies is tantamount to alienation from one's self. Third, for Marx creative activity was not a contingent characteristic but the very essence of human nature, or what he called "species being." In Deweyan terms, a species that could not create solutions to the problems that arise in its interactions with its environment would perish. Consequently, artistic alienation is ultimately alienation from human nature. Loss of creative autonomy can be dehumanizing. Finally, competition, enforced perhaps by norm referenced performance testing, not only oppresses us but alienates us from our fellow artist. Merit pay systems are an example. In their conclusion, McCloskey et al. (1991) state that "teachers identified here as negative about legislated learning feel alienated by the mandated policies" (p. 263). Marx helps us see the existential depths of such alienation.

Scientific technique in the service of the state's disciplinary technology reduces the possibility for intelligent action by demanding conformity to pre-established means specified in detail in the form of procedures, rules, and regulations. Artistic creative autonomy is reduced when teachers are forced to accept predetermined ends such as "teacher proof" curriculums. Finally, if Whitehead is correct, the sphere for moral action is reduced when teachers are unable to fashion and restrain their power to attain their foreseen and desired ends. Without a sense of style, there is no internal motivation to prefer good work. Morality, in terms of internal responsibility for one's actions carried out to achieve ends with which we are personally identified, gives way to mere legality; that is, conformity to externally imposed codes and standards. The reduction of morality to legality, and mere rule following, completes the reduction of existential meaning and value that results from the excessive and misdirected application of any disciplinary technology, including the teachers' own classroom disciplinary system, however desirable and necessary it may be when properly used.

So far, we have been discussing the vices of the scientific technique. I would now like to turn to the virtues of the scientific temper. The scientific temper will turn out to be an important part of the aesthetic of a powerful and effective style.

Returning to Raitz and Fenstermacher will help us better draw out the subtle distinction between the scientific technique and the scientific temper. Raitz is right, I think, in asserting that there are no techniques taken as mere value neutral means. Where he is mistaken is concluding from that that "generic teaching technique is rationally indefensible" (Raitz, 1989, p. 56). Fenstermacher is on target when he says that there are generic teaching methods. For instance, it is generally a good idea to begin class promptly and for teachers to keep themselves and their students on task. Significantly, though, it is a general method of *inquiry* adequate for everything from investigating a classroom behavioral problem to finding a grand unifying theory of forces in physics that most interested Dewey. Fenstermacher goes a bit too far, though, when he defends the existence of detached techniques. His own example seems to be a counter example to his claim. Fenstermacher finds that, "Such detachment is evident in the novice piano player practicing chords" (p. 64). It seems to me that any piano player practices chords for the purpose of fashioning their power and professional proficiency for achieving their end, i.e., a fine performance. A detached technique, as Raitz defined it, would involve *doing* chords for no purpose at all. Or one could do chords for discipline, like writing "I will not tear up the test" one thousand times on the blackboard. It is certainly possible to detach and reattach a set of behaviors to a new purpose, but doing so gives them a new meaning and value. They are no longer the same thing. For example, a Florida teacher once told me that when the Florida Performance Measurement System evaluator was in her classroom she was not teaching, rather, she was giving a dramatic performance. She didn't *teach* like that. Random behaviors are meaningless unless we interpret them in terms of some purpose. In a disciplinary technology like that described by Foucault, those higher up on the hierarchy usually have the power to determine the "true" interpretation. That is what "power/knowledge" is all about. It is the performance evaluator that will decide when eye contact becomes glaring, suspicious, or shows anger.

Dewey identified three sources of the scientific technique. The first was the powerful tendency to "start from general principles" and rules secured by abstract principles of "pure reason" rather than "scientific generalizations" that are "subject to revision as inquiry proceeds" (Dewey, 1946, p. 172). Second, Dewey believed that the scientific technique represented "the essential capture of the technical resources of the new science" by "finance-capital" and "political nationalism" (p. 174). I believe these forces are still at work in the current reform movement in teaching and teacher education. Finally, Dewey (1946) sees the scientific technique as a rather unintelligent response to "the modern danger of chaos and anarchy" (p. 175). The technocratic disciplinary technology described by Foucault is a fine example of meeting the postmodern, postindustrial, and now post-cold-war chaos and anarchy by some form of external and dogmatic authority rather than freeing creative intelligence—the virtues of the scientific temper. These are the virtues that Raitz thinks are destroyed by detached technique. They are the virtues of what Dewey called "the method of intelligence."

Dewey on General and Individual Method: "Intelligence and Character"

What Dewey meant by the method of intelligence cannot be detached either from desired results (i.e., purposes) or from specific subject matter materials. Dewey is explicitly thinking about pedagogy here; his example is instructive. Dewey (1916a) wrote:

> Every artist must have a method, a technique, in doing his work. Piano playing is not hitting the keys at random. Order is found in the disposition of acts which use the piano and the hands and brain so as to achieve the result intended. It is the action of the piano directed to accomplish the purpose of the piano as a musical instrument. It is the same with "pedagogical" method. . . . Method in any case is but an effective way of employing some material for some end. (p. 172)

Style is teleological. The person who possesses style is also possessed by the intended result they seek. The teacher possessed of pedagogical style creatively organizes curriculum materials, the subject matter, class time, their students' needs and desires, their own strengths and weaknesses, and much more to achieve their ends and only their ends. In order to achieve their purposes every artist must have methods and techniques to do their work. Intelligent method is inseparable from a fine pedagogical performance. It is an instrument for gracefully fashioning and restraining power in order to achieve a desired outcome. It is an important part of professionalism. Methods, general and individual, are the tools of style.

An important section of Dewey's chapter on method in *Democracy and Education* (1916a; 1980) is subtitled "Method as General and as Individual" (p. 177). Dewey began this subsection explicitly connecting methods of teaching to art. Dewey wrote, "the method of teaching is the method of an art, of action intelligently directed by ends" (p. 177). The idea of art being *directed* by ends was important for Dewey. For Dewey "ends-in-view," provided not only Whitehead's foresight, "the last gift of gods to men," but a practical plan of action for achieving the desired end. Style requires method.

Like other arts Dewey concluded:

> Education also has its general methods....These general methods are in no way opposed to individual initiative and originality—to personal ways of doing things. On the contrary they are reinforcements of them. For there is a radical difference between even the most general method and a prescribed rule. The latter is a *direct* guide to action; the former operates indirectly through the enlightenment it supplies as to ends and means. It operates that is to say, through intelligence, and not through conformity to orders externally imposed. (p. 178)

Prescribed methodological rules and standards externally imposed limit the scope of intelligent action and response. Such mandates are no doubt intended to limit bad practice, but they are perhaps just as frequently a cause of malpractice. Dewey is also making an important epistemological as well as practical point. As Dewey (1916a; 1980) affirmed "after all cases are *like*, not identical. To be used intelligently, existing practices however authorized they may be, have to be adapted to the exigencies of particular cases" (p. 178). The epistemological point is that even if we had all of the right methods on our shelves, we would still be confronted with the problem of identifying *this* particular case as an instance amendable to this method. That is to say, we would have to interpret the situation correctly, and that requires style. Practically, no two cases are identical; individuals will have to adapt methods to fit the case identified. Finally, the individual, with their talents and limitations, are always part of the case and must be included in all practical considerations of methodology. It is impossible to generalize a particular case beyond a certain point. It is here that individual method becomes important.

Regarding the general features of a reflective experience Dewey (1916a; 1980) stated:

> They are: (i) perplexity, confusion, doubt, due to the fact that one is implicated in an incomplete situation [a problem] whose full character is not yet determined; (ii) a conjectural anticipation—a tentative interpretation of the given elements, attributing to them a tendency to effect certain consequences; (iii) a careful survey (examination, inspection, exploration, analysis) of all attainable consideration which will define and clarify the problem in hand; (iv) a consequent elaboration of the tentative hypothesis to make it more precise and more consistent, because squaring with a wider range of facts; (v) taking one's stand upon the projected hypothesis as a plan of action.... (p. 157)

The most general features of the reflective situation should be in the possession of all teachers since it would empower them to carry out inquiries, e.g., action research, to solve their own problems by fashioning their classrooms to meet their own ends.

Let us now turn to what Dewey meant by individual methods since it is these that will lead most directly to the morality of the individual teacher's mind. Dewey (1916a; 1980) prefaced his discussion of some of the traits of individual method with the following remarks:

> The specific elements of an individual's method or way of attack upon a problem are found ultimately in his (sic) native tendencies and his acquired habits and interests. The method of one will vary from that of another (and *properly* vary) as his original instinctive capacities vary, as his past experiences and his preferences vary....But methods remain the personal concern, approach and attack of an individual, and no catalogue can ever exhaust their diversity of form and tint....Some attitudes may be named, however, which are central in effective intellectual ways of dealing with subject

matter. Among the most important are directness, open-mindedness, single-mindedness. . .and responsibility. (p. 180)

It is important to note that Dewey is restraining himself to intelligent ways of dealing with subject matter. The traits of individual method are the intellectual virtues specific to an individual's engagement in a reflective situation and using methods of knowing. Further, it is important to note that the list of traits is open ended and that Dewey only discussed some of those that he saw as central.

The first trait is directness, by which Dewey meant a concentration of effort and energy. Negatively, "Self-consciousness, embarrassment, and constraint are its menacing foes. They indicate that a person is not immediately concerned with subject matter. Something has come between which deflects concern to side issues" (Dewey, 1916a; 1980, p. 180). The power of one's style to fashion a successful outcome in a situation is enhanced if it is focused on the subject matter rather than on oneself, others, or something else. Confidence is another term Dewey uses to describe directedness. By confidence Dewey does not mean *self*-confidence. Instead, confidence "denotes not *conscious* trust in the efficacy of one's powers but unconscious faith in the possibilities of the situation. It signifies rising to the needs of the situation" (Dewey, 1916a; 1980, p. 181).

Next comes "open-mindedness." This trait is "an attitude of mind which actively welcomes suggestions and relevant information from all sides. . .foreseen ends are factors in the development of a changing situation. . . .They are, as foreseen, *means* of guiding the development of a situation" (Dewey, 1916a; 1980, p. 182, italics in original). Open-mindedness is open to the possibilities, including those offered by other persons, in some problematic situation. Whitehead felt that those who had style had foresight. If Dewey is right, then foresight comes to those who are open-minded. Negatively, Dewey notes that "Exorbitant desire for uniformity of procedure and for prompt external results are the chief foes which the open-minded attitude meets in school" (p. 182). Dewey continued on to make a subtle distinction when he remarked "Open-mindedness is not the same as empty-mindedness. To hang out a sign saying 'come right in; there is no one at home' is not the equivalent of hospitality" (p. 183). Compare this statement with what A. G. Rud has to say elsewhere in this collection of essays on gaps in the moral conversation about comfort and trust in teaching, and the importance of listening to strangers, as well as the strangeness within ourselves. As I will suggest in the conclusion, style is a political virtue composed itself of many virtues. Rud is right to associate hospitality as preparation for inviting and receiving others as a political virtue that contributes to a democratic political involvement.

The third trait is "single-mindedness." It overlaps directness and expresses the absence of ulterior motive, external motivation, or reward. Single-mindedness attains its ends, and only its ends, without raising undesirable inflammations or distracted irrelevances. It is an element of style. Single-mindedness might be called "moral efficiency."

Dewey (1916a; 1980) straightforwardly defines what he means by responsibility:

> By responsibility. . . is meant the disposition to consider in advance the probable consequences of any projected step and deliberately to accept them: to accept them in the sense of taking them into account, acknowledging them in action, not yielding a mere verbal assent. Ideas, as we have seen, are intrinsically standpoints and methods for bringing about a solution of a perplexing situation. . . (p. 185)

The gift of foresight permits possible, but not actual, "ends-in-view" to guide present actual action because the teacher believes that such circumstances *ought* to exist, places the onus of responsibility on that teacher not only for the consequences obtained by action, but those unobtained by inaction, or the failure to be properly informed. As Whitehead (1929; 1967) understood it, "Duty arises from our potential control over the course of events. Where attainable knowledge could have changed the issue, ignorance has the guilt of vice" (p. 14). "Duty" is an intellectual virtue closely related to responsibility. Duty and responsibility are the required restraints on the power of individual style to fashion its desired ends.

We have seen how Dewey connects the general methods of inquiry, knowledge acquisition, and learning with traits of individual *artistic* endeavors to act intelligently to achieve desired ends. We should not be surprised that Dewey, the arch antidualist, eventually connected the cognitive and artistic with the ethical. In the concluding chapter of *Democracy and Education*, titled "Theories of Morals" Dewey (1916a; 1980) declared:

> the qualities of mind discussed under the topic of method of learning are all of them intrinsically *moral* qualities. Open-mindedness, single-mindedness, sincerity, breadth of outlook, thoroughness, assumption of responsibility for developing the consequences of ideas which are accepted, are moral traits. The

habit of identifying moral characteristics with external conformity to authoritative prescriptions [rules and principles] may
lead us to ignore the ethical value of these intellectual attitudes,
but the same habit tends to reduce morals to a dead and
machine-like routine. Consequently while such an attitude has
moral results, the results are morally undesirable—above all in
a democratic society where so much depends upon personal
disposition. (pp. 366–367, italics added)

By refusing to separate method from subject matter, and by defining
methods in terms of organizing the subject matter for a purpose, Dewey
seeks to block the attempt to separate theory and practice. All reasoning
for Dewey was practical means-ends reasoning, and he connected the
application of cognitive methods to artistic creativity and both to
individual traits of moral character. We will take up the connection
between intrinsic moral qualities, external control, and democracy in
our conclusion.

Style is destroyed by the disciplinary technology of bureaucratic
and technocratic thinking. Similar remarks could be made about the
other "gaps" introduced in this volume. In my conclusion I want to
discuss why Dewey's connection of moral traits, that I have suggested
are also traits of style, to issues of external conformity to authority and
issues of democratic society is not mistaken. Style as the ultimate
morality of the mind is bound to have political implications.

Conclusion: Style, Postmodernity, and Politics

I would like to conclude with a suggestion as to why individual style
may indeed be the ultimate morality of the mind, at least if we take
morality as being concerned with our conduct toward others. Dewey
(1916a; 1980) explicitly acknowledged the importance of social control
functions throughout *Democracy and Education* (see, for example, pp.
31–32), in ways that do anticipate aspects of Foucault. He was also
explicit about the importance of the private creative functions as well,
"Every *new* idea, every conception of things differing from that
authorized by current belief, must have its origin in an individual. New
ideas are doubtless always sprouting, but a society governed by custom
does not encourage their development" (p. 305). An important act of
creation is self-creation in the sense of getting out from under the
massive weight of tradition, custom, to dig out of a whole mass of
accumulated discourse, as Foucault described it. Irony, tragedy, and
good luck will be always be required. To stop believing what our parents,
friends, and nation tells us is painful, and oftentimes a mistake.

Ironically, it is only after we have reconstructed the "self" assigned us by our culture that we can truly say we have a "mind" of our own. Only then can we be truly said to have style. Individually we can recreate ourselves and others, but we can never escape our culture.

If Dewey is correct, then alienation of the kind discussed earlier not only existentially harms the private person by destroying their ability to function creatively, but in the dialectic of the private and public, it deprives the public of the needed products of free individual creative intelligence. If so, then the alienation of teachers, i.e., the destruction of the psychic rewards of teaching including creative autonomy, is not simply a matter of teachers not feeling good and burning out thereby creating retention problems. It deprives public education of the products of free creative intelligence; it is profoundly unprofitable.

Private acts of creation, be they inquiries like Alexander Fleming's discovery of penicillin, productions like Igor Stravinsky's "The Rite of Spring," constructions of statecraft, like Thomas Jefferson's *A Bill For Establishing Religious Freedom* (an innovative idea later ensconced in the Constitution of the United States of America), or Mrs. Good, my twelfth grade history teacher, whose methods created in me an enduring love of her subject matter, all alter social relations and affect other human beings. Individual acts of creation always carry a moral commitment; for the artist is saying that this thing, person or state of affairs *ought* to exist in *our* world. And so we are brought to Dewey's, and I must admit my own, deep faith that there is, at least at this point in human evolution, a system of social relations best suited to working out the dialectically related functions of public social control and private creativity.

Dewey's faith in democracy led him to have a deep concern for education, i.e., the education of experience. Now let us become clear as to what he meant by democracy. In *Democracy and Education* Dewey (1916a; 1980) wrote:

A democracy is more than a form of government; it is primarily a mode of associated living, of conjoint communicated experience. The extension in space of the number of individuals who participate in an interests so that each has to refer his own action to that of others, and to consider the action of others to give point and direction to his own, is equivalent to the breaking down of those barriers of class, race, and national territory which kept men from perceiving the full import of their activity. These more numerous and more varied points of contact . . . secure a liberation of powers which remain suppressed as long

as the incitations to action are partial, as they must be in a group
which in its exclusiveness shuts out many interests. (p. 93)

Democracy in Dewey's opinion is the most logical form of governance
because it facilitates dialogue, that is, associated living and conjoint
communicated experience in which all participants must refer their
actions, including their creative actions, to that of others.

Now think about the classroom teacher at the bottom of the
hierarchy of disciplinary technology described by Foucault. In modern
American education teachers are literally talked down to in the
disciplinary hierarchy. The result of legislated learning is that ideas are
not communicated, shared, and reborn in expression. Instead, teachers
receive a soliloquy, and soliloquy is but broken and imperfect thought.
Social relations in American schools are dominated by the merely
technical *interests* of the scientific technique. The results are not only
illogical, they are ultimately also undemocratic. Such social relations
do not allow the development of individual style. And without style,
I have tried to show, there can be no strong sense of oneself as a creative
and competent craftsperson, an empowered professional, or a visionary
leader taking students to novel ends in view. Style may not be the
ultimate morality of the mind, but it is among the most important
qualities any practitioner can possess because it expresses so many
professional virtues. Any system, and that includes virtually all of the
current proposals for educational reform, that destroys style is not only
immoral, it is an unprofitable mistake for which there is no accounting.

CHAPTER 5

Pragmatism and the Ironic Teacher of Virtue

Alven Neiman

I

It is not merely a coincidence that Socrates, one of the West's greatest teachers, was an ironist. His irony, expressed not simply as a way of speaking but as a manner of living, was essential to his educational strategy and style. Moreover, the example of a number of other great moral teachers reminds us that irony has often been a key ingredient in education. Jesus Christ, Søren Kierkegaard, Jonathan Swift, Martin Buber in his depiction of Hasidic masters, George Orwell—the list of ironic teachers of virtue is long and distinguished. Thus, it should at least initially puzzle us that today educational theorists, philosophers, and practitioners seldom, if ever, sing the praises of irony. Why, then, is it now so neglected by today's teachers and teacher educators? Surely it is not just because it involves using words to express something other, and often the opposite, of what the words seem to mean literally. In writing this chapter I want to recommend a certain kind of pragmatic irony as a response to the contingencies and uncertainties of the postmodern classroom.

The dangers of irony are well recognized within our educational tradition. It has always been recognized that irony can be misused or misunderstood, but today it seems that irony is more and more often viewed as *essentially* corrupting. Take irony and follow its natural progression, it is thought, and the result is nihilism. As in Nietzsche's reading, follow Socrates along his ironic pathway and one reaches a point of ultimate decadence, catalogued at the end of the *Phaedo*, where life itself can only appear to be an illness. Follow Swift, or at least Gulliver, along the ironic path of *Gulliver's Travels* and reach book IV, where in a state of horror we discover that we are incurable Yahoos, tragically given just enough clarity of vision in the story of the Houyhnhnms to be tortured by our inescapable failure to live as they do. In the grip of this fear of irony we turn our great ironists into

61

creatures of reassuring earnestness, creatures whose irony is merely ornamental. We forget how strange, how bizarre, how frightening Socrates must have been to his fellow citizens. We make *Gulliver's Travels* into a children's tale (and generally leave out the tale of the Houyhnhnms and Yahoos). We ignore evidence to the contrary in the Gospels and turn Jesus into a sweet, nurturing savior. In doing so, we ought to remember that these revisions imply losses as well as gains.

Good examples of the sort of worry about irony that I am concerned about are to be found in recent criticism of the work of the neo-pragmatic philosopher Richard Rorty who writes in the Deweyan pragmatic tradition. Rorty's (1989) book, *Contingency, Irony, and Solidarity,* implicitly contains a series of educational proposals that make irony into a major virtue to be taught to inhabitants of an ideal liberal democracy. This society would be ideal in part because its best educated citizens would be pragmatists rather than Philosophers (with a capital *P*). As such, these citizens would give up the Philosophical search for Truth, Goodness, Reality, and Rationality that has, according to Rorty, defined the Western philosophical tradition since Plato. There are for Rorty no eternal essences and timeless truths.[1] For him nothing is ever certain. Past and present philosophy, in his words, continues the "...attempt to step outside our skins—the traditions, linguistic and others, within which we do our thinking and self-criticism—and compare ourselves with something absolute" (Rorty, 1982, p. xix). Philosophy aims to step outside of finitude and contingency to grasp the essence of things, the one true transcendental metanarrative that would mirror "how things are." The pragmatist would part from this tradition in order to make a new start.

Rorty's pragmatist substitutes for the foundationalist theory of knowledge a vision of knowledge as coping, as action in practical pursuit of the fulfillment of various goods particular human beings cherish at one time or another. From the perspective of traditional philosophy, he looks like someone who gives up the Platonic quest for certainty about Reality in order to remain content within the cave of culture, choosing (ironically enough) to remain satisfied with the examination of various forms of life, various caves of culture in an attempt to live wisely and well. In response to the philosopher, pragmatists argue "...that the history of attempts to isolate the True or the Good...supports their suspicion that there is no interesting work to be done in this area" (Rorty, 1982, p. xiv). In short, the pragmatist wants to give up traditional Philosophy in order to go on living without the illusions fostered in the West by the quest for certainty.

In *Contingency, Irony, and Solidarity* Rorty argues that at least the most favored of these ideal citizens, these pragmatists, would be ironists. Thus, in this book Rorty is implicitly suggesting that irony would be *an* important aim of such a society's educational system, if only at its highest level. Elsewhere I have tried to make some of those implicit suggestions explicit, tried to explain what Rorty's pragmatic ironist might look like, and how an education for such irony might proceed (see Neiman, 1991). Here I want to extend that account but, more fundamentally, concentrate on criticisms of Rorty that suggest that irony is in fact an undesirable quality, that educators should *not* see it as an aim of education.

Critics of Rorty's ironist exemplify these worries. Writers like Sheldon Wolin (1990), Michael Quirk (1991), and Richard Bernstein (1990) constantly refer to Rorty's ironist as necessarily a relativist or nihilist. For Wolin, for example, such an ironist rejects all the healthy values of our Western enlightenment tradition fostered by Philosophy, in favor of an egocentric and self-destructive aestheticism. Their worry is that irony in this postmodern mode is the last thing we need to pass on to our young.

These worries about irony are implicitly related to an educational context in Allan Bloom's (1987) *The Closing of the American Mind*. Bloom worries that our universities already produce people that, like their teachers, resemble these critics' picture of Rortyan ironists as "cheerful nihilists" resembling Ivan Karamazovs prior to their self-recognition and descent into horror. Bloom's writings can be taken to codify contemporary worries about an academic system ruled by "tenured radicals" who would teach irony rather than philosophy. Bloom's book can be read, in this context, as a plea that irony be always tethered to Philosophy, and as a warning against emphasizing irony in cultural and educational contexts in which philosophy is undergoing serious attack. *The Closing of the American Mind* can be read, in this way, as proposing as a cure for current cultural and educational sickness the earnestness of traditional philosophy, with its assurance of certainty and decontextualized rational rules and laws, against an untethered postmodern irony.

My way of responding to such critics will be as follows. In the next section, I want to discuss exactly what Rorty's irony amounts to, and very briefly set his picture of the liberal ironist within the context of education in the Utopian liberal society. In a third and fourth sections, I will discuss several works of literary philosophy, Plato's *Symposium* and Milan Kundera's *The Unbearable Lightness of Being*, in order to describe Plato's Socrates and Kundera's Sabina as types of ironist. Within this setting I will, in later sections, seek to situate Rorty's liberal ironist so as to provide a response to the sorts of criticisms discussed in this section.

I will not, in what follows, remain a slavish devotee of Rorty's viewpoint. Perhaps the best way to understand my ongoing project is as an attempt to rationally reconstruct the Rortyan ironist in such a way as to create an educationally viable ideal type of teacher and teacher educator. Like Rorty, I will assume that the type of education to be discussed is one meant for the best educated person in a liberal society. Moreover, I will, in what follows, remain devoted to the pragmatic viewpoint. Rorty says we must constantly look to the consequences of our ideas and acts to fix their meaning and test their truth (lower case *t*) in a constantly changing and contingent world. Thus, the question of this essay becomes: can we today make sense of, make defensible against criticism, the pragmatic ironist as an ideal educational type?

II

All of us know how much trouble the use of irony caused Socrates and, thus, the cause of philosophy. It led to his execution by the democratic state. As teachers and teacher educators, we think of his use of irony in questioning various Athenians about their beliefs and lives, and we recall its seemingly corrosive effect among the decadent aristocratic youth of Athens. In questioning people Socrates' irony evokes bitterness and woe; in this context, we wonder whether his jury might have been more temperate with him if he had treated them less ironically. Even his loves, like Alcibiades as described in the *Symposium*, fall prey to an irony that breeds misunderstanding, and, thus, pain. Since the time of Socrates, the majority of philosophers, chastened by his example, have seemingly resisted irony. Instead of following the example of Socrates the enigmatic ironist, they have made Plato, apparently the champion of metaphysics, Truth, and total explanation, their hero.

Thus, Richard Rorty should have known how people, in general, would respond (badly, of course) to his irony. In this section I want to talk explicitly about Rorty's irony, about his view of the relationship of his irony to his politics, and, in conclusion, about how such ideas reflect pedagogical concerns. In later sections I begin the task of defending pragmatic views on these matters, views inspired by but not equivalent to Rorty's, from the kind of criticism discussed in section I.

First of all, what, for Rorty, does irony amount to? In *Contingency, Irony, and Solidarity*, he distinguishes the ironist, as an ideal type, from both the common sensist and the metaphysician.[2] He begins his discussion of these types by noting that each of us in our thinking and acting necessarily makes use of a "final vocabulary," a conceptual network embodying a complex set of beliefs, attitudes, and orientations that ground our enactment of who we are. The ironist, says Rorty, is someone who comes to understand that even our most basic beliefs are not indubitable, incorrigible, or in short, known with certainty, or known at all. Rather, what we think of ourselves and our world as well as what we do, is *radically* contingent upon our place in history and society. The common sensist educator responds to this recognition of contingency by denying it, by insisting that the worries of the ironist's all-inclusive view of things is less than fully warranted are radically misguided.

The metaphysician takes the fact of contingency more seriously than the common sensist, suggesting that our now rather arbitrary foundation of knowledge must somehow be connected to a necessary one, legislated by the way the world and the self "really" is. Thus the Philosopher Descartes tries to build a truly philosophical foundation of knowledge by setting aside all that is merely contingent, or a Plato tries to discover a reality of knowledge or science beyond luck and fortune.

The ironist has radical doubts about the project of the metaphysician and no longer thinks of language as a medium between some mythical external "Reality" and internal belief or thought; the ironist despairs of the idea of "Truth" and "Universal laws" as a property of representative beliefs or thoughts. The ironist, thus understood, is not merely a fallibilist, not merely someone who knows that in our search for knowledge we can at best obtain mere probability, intelligent belief that may need revision sometime in the future. It is not simply that the ironist realizes that the most reliable beliefs and values may thus fall short of the mark. Rather the very idea of "the mark," a "Reality" that one's thought or language may or may not get right, is, for Rorty, called into question. The ironist "knows," perhaps from studying Dewey's (1929, p. 198) *The Quest for Certainty* or Wittgenstein's (1969) *On Certainty* that all living and acting requires the acceptance of basic beliefs in a way akin to certainty. Yet the ironist also "knows" that one cannot intend this certainty as a foundationalist believer in timeless Truths might. The "knowledge" is exhibited in the rhetoric of irony, in the awareness that must mean something different than what says (and perhaps what one does).

So the ironist, even with justification or warrant of common sense or metaphysics, lives and breathes, acts as a "being in the world," where commitment, at the very least to confidently held sets of beliefs and values, is required. As the philosopher (lower case *p*) Ludwig Wittgenstein showed, doubt, belief, life itself requires a bedrock of certainty, but the ironist understands this certainty as problematic. It is not simply that the ironist believes that it is unwarranted in lieu of a justified metaphysics. Rather, the ironist understands oneself to be in a position where ones very life intimates the kind of assertions of "Truths" about "Reality" that cannot, if pragmatism is right, be taken literally.

In its philosophical mode Rorty's irony is, I believe, suggestive of William James's pragmatism and radical empiricism, where language and theory become instruments and what philosophers have traditionally called "Reality" is seen as intrinsically pluralistic, i.e., irreducible to any one discourse or point of view. Within this vision "True Reality" is (to mimic the phrasing in another context, of my colleague David O'Connor) ". . . seen more as a locus of dispersion for a discourse (to borrow a phrase from Michel Foucault) than a stable and unified focal point, more a mystery than a puzzle to be solved."[3]

In *Contingency, Irony, and Solidarity,* Rorty makes use of such ideas, among others, to argue for a Utopian society in which a character he calls "the liberal ironist" becomes the ideal. In his preface, Rorty (1989) describes this character as an ironist whose final vocabulary embodies certain elements of traditional liberal ideology, e.g., the desire that above all else individual suffering and humiliation must cease. In order to defend the habit of irony against critics who see irony as destructive of liberal ideas, he resorts to what he describes as a "firm distinction" between a private realm (or ironic self-formation) and a public realm (of politics). Thus, he speaks of irony as "invaluable in our attempt to form a private self-image but pretty much useless when it comes to politics" (Rorty, 1989, pp. 84, 87).

I am unhappy with this response to the liberal attack on irony. I applaud Rorty for contesting claims that a partisan of liberal politics cannot truly be an ironist. But (and here is the irony I promised you early on) I believe he does not go far enough. I want to suggest not merely that the ironic temper can coexist with liberalism and liberal teaching and learning, but that it can be seen as an important part of a liberal political temperament.

In order to approach my thesis with any sympathy at all, I believe we must stop thinking, in the way Rorty does, of anti-liberals like Nietzsche as paradigmatic ironists. For this reason I, in my account of Rorty's irony, refer not to these philosophers but, instead, to the earlier pragmatic philosopher William James. I wish Rorty had specifically made use of James, instead of writers like Nietzsche, when he wrote about irony. If he had, he might have been less inclined to give credence to the complaints that a partisan of liberal politics cannot be an ironist, and others, concerning the opposition of irony and liberal community. I am aware of James's fear, a fear also found in his mentor Ralph Waldo Emerson, that society, in its political or economic phase, can only hinder the self as the locus of freedom and value. But as a pragmatist I am also aware of the achievement of Dewey in reconciling the Jamesian concern for individual self-formation with a proper appreciation of scientific intelligence and democracy as social achievements. I take Dewey's works as evidence that Jamesian irony is not necessarily antithetical to true community. Irony, in fact, can best be understood as at least one final cause of liberal education for citizenship in such a community; for example, the professional teacher genuinely participating in a decentralized site-based and democratically managed school.

What would education look like in such a community? Rorty's description, in a number of essays, of a two-part process, first of socialization and then of self-creation, strikes me as providing a pretty good response to this question.[4] Rorty (1989) is right, in *Contingency, Irony, and Solidarity*, to insist that education cannot begin in irony, since irony is essentially reactive against beliefs taken as certainties (pp. 87 ff). Initially, beginning teachers *do* need some secure laws, rules, and principles that work well practically in most classroom situations. It is here that research programs like Lee Shulman's may pay off. Teachers need the security and confidence to cope. But some sorts of socialization are, it seems to me, more amenable to a later stage of irony than others. In the kind of community I am imagining, socialization into a liberal tradition of increasing tolerance of philosophical and practical differences will lead rather naturally, at least among those truly willing and able to be liberally educated, into an educational phase in which communal intelligence, understood as essentially involving Socratic and Jamesian irony, becomes possible. Certain kinds of discourse, taken in early on in life or in one's teacher preparation program, makes irony easier to achieve.

But come now, can irony really be so basic to any sort of politics? Isn't irony, untempered by the stability and earnestness of common sense or metaphysics, by the fundamental clarity these ways of being offer us, in reality corrosive of all human solidarity, all human community? In the context of these questions I want to begin to imagine a community of persons who, in their irony, are willing to reject the kind of salvation offered in educational and political dogmas and theories taken as more or less accurate representations of social reality.

I want to imagine, that is, a community of ironists willing to treat nature and others as James meant to, as mysteries rather than puzzles to be solved, as beings too important to enslave within theory taken without irony. I see this outlook as capable of breeding common purpose, as engendering respect and awe rather than intolerance or manipulation. I see, in short, this Jamesian paradise as the proper culmination of Rorty's neo-pragmatic vision, unencumbered by the faddishness of continental apolitical nihilism. Here I believe is a vision of a community in which Socrates need not be martyred, and in which the philosophical irony of a Richard Rorty might find a welcome suitable to its noble lineage.

Later I want to return to this Jamesian vision, in order to begin to discuss it at greater length. But now I return to face the critics of pragmatic irony. In order to do this I will, in good Rortyan fashion, turn more to the discussion of literary texts than to an attempt at pure, decontextualized, philosophical argument. In order to illustrate a traditional view of philosophically valuable irony stabilized by metaphysics, I begin with a discussion of the role of irony in Plato's *Symposium*. There (at least on traditional readings) it seems that Plato frees Socrates' irony from charges of irresponsibility by tethering it to an idyllic world of forms. Socrates' corrosive irony is thus rendered acceptable through its service to "The Good." There, in the *Symposium*, Socrates becomes pre-pragmatic irony personified; he mirrors the duality of a world in which eros, the motivating force of passion within us, strives to transcend the incomplete, finite, and temporal in order to attain the complete, infinite, and permanent. Like the critic of Rorty discussed above, I want to ask what happens to such irony in a time like ours, a time in which belief in such Platonic ideals is hard to come by?

My discussion of the work of novelist Milan Kundera is meant immediately to suggest a rather dismal answer to this question.[5] Kundera, in novels such as *The Unbearable Lightness of Being*, can be seen to suggest that world of the Platonic Idyll and other absolutes must for us pragmatists be an unreflective commitment to uncertainty. In this world irony seems to become, in the words of Francois Ricard (1987), satanic, a mode of radical demystification that leaves behind nothing but "...the eternal and derisory empire of accident and error." In the world of this novel, well characterized in the heroic "Saint Sabina," it seems that irony must become a purely nihilistic device. Nihilism, it is often claimed, is the inevitable consequence of conceding that everything is contingent and changing.

It is in this dismal context that I will attempt to resurrect pragmatic irony, to show that such irony can avoid nihilism.

III

Why is Socrates, as portrayed in the Platonic dialogue, ironic? What is the point of his irony and what are its dangers? How can such dangers be overcome so as to render irony safe and stable? It seems that even in the time of Plato visions of Socrates were essentially contested. Ideas of Socrates as primordial cynic or skeptic, later to be developed and promoted within various schools of Greek philosophy, must have already been prevalent. Aristophanes' portrayal of Socrates, in *The Clouds*, as a rather crass, bumbling yet shrewd Sophist, capable of persuading anyone of anything, must have at least to some extent mirrored the truth in order to service such an effective parody. To understand Plato's portrayal of Socrates, perhaps it is best to view it in the light of a controversy, over the essential meaning, intent, and scope of Socratic irony, and over the proper value and use of irony *per se*.

The times must have resembled ours at least in one crucial respect. The worries educators confront today concerning irony can, I think, be related to what Richard Bernstein in a recent book refers to as Cartesian anxiety. Yet such anxiety is at least as old as Plato and Socrates. Bernstein discusses the well known crisis of objectivity in our learned professions, and perhaps in large parts of our culture as well. He notes that from Plato onward in the West, an objectivist tradition has insisted that life can be satisfactory only if "...there are...fixed permanent constraints to which we can appeal and which are secure and stable." The crisis of objectivity, Bernstein (1983) notes, is based on

> ...the growing apprehension that there may be nothing—not God, reason, philosophy, science or poetry—that answers to and satisfies our longing for ultimate constraints, for a stable and reliable rock upon which we can secure our thought and action. (p. 9)

I have already suggested that our reluctance to take irony seriously as a way of education for ourselves and our students stems from our worry that, in the absence of such constraints, it takes its natural course towards profoundly anti-educational results, such as personal despair and general cultural malaise. I believe something like this crisis of objectivity existed for the genteel class of Greeks in Plato's time is well documented. Plato's way of rendering irony safe and stable, as well as any difficulty we may have in taking that way very seriously, point to the problems and projects facing anyone who would today attempt to resurrect irony as a valuable educational aim and device.

In dialogues like the *Symposium*, it is clear that Plato understands the dangers of irony. His resolution to any doubts or dangers he might have had about irony, at least in this dialogue, involves him in drawing an essential connection between it and his metaphysical constraints, the forms. In the *Symposium*, Plato views Socrates' irony, powered by eros, that is, passionate desire, as serving the form of forms, and eternal and immutable "The Good." Not even the broken lives of students such as Alcibiades can legitimately call such service into question. Not even Alcibiades' misunderstandings of that irony cause the Socrates of the *Symposium* to leave irony alone. The *Symposium*, as well as any modern (or postmodern) document, demonstrates what is at stake for education in the battle over irony.

A major concern of Gregory Vlastos (1991) in his recent discussion of irony in the *Symposium* is whether Socrates meant to deceive Alcibiades. Alcibiades falters, Vlastos suggests, because he fails to understand that the Socratic claims concerning wisdom, ignorance or eros are to be taken as cases of what Vlastos calls complex irony. In simple cases of irony one asserts something to be the case but literally intends the opposite; so a teacher, chastising a student performing poorly in class might say to the student "you're doing a brilliant job." In complex irony, however, what irony intends is more than simple negation; it aims at a new understanding beyond the conventional meanings of our words and deeds or our final vocabulary. Socrates' irony in his claim to wisdom requires that he is known not to be wise in the conventional sense. On the surface level complex irony presents obvious falsehood; but in its enigmatic presentation it points towards a deeper reality. Socrates is wise, but not in the conventional sense; his wisdom will seem strange or bizarre to those like Agathon, who think of wisdom as similar to water which can be poured from one vessel to another. It is a wisdom beyond knowledge alone. To take another example, Socrates speaks truly when he says he loves Alcibiades and other Athenian youths such as Agathon. But the literal-minded, who equate love with physical attraction and consummation, can only be confused or angered by such claims. And the young Alcibiades, who is described in the *Symposium* as having pursued Socratic wisdom, is both confused and angry.

So of what value is Socratic irony if it has such effects? Why doesn't Socrates, who surely is aware that his irony has often been misunderstood, simply tell Alcibiades the *literal* truth? Vlastos concludes that Socrates wants Alcibiades to know the truth but, more importantly, he wants him, and others, to come to the truth by themselves through critical reflection and thought. In this way Vlastos believes that a response can be provided to those who accuse Socrates of irresponsibility in his refusal to communicate non-ironically to his students so as to provide answers to his own questions. Wisdom cannot, it seems, be poured out of Socrates into a passive Thrasymachus, Alcibiades, or anyone else. It must be struggled for and won only after a hard-fought battle. Souls must turn toward wisdom for themselves.

It is important at this point to remember that in the *Symposium* it is an older, wiser Alcibiades that recalls his earlier defeats at the hand of Socrates. This older Alcibiades has to some extent caught on; he says of Socrates, "In public, I tell you, his whole life is one big game—one big game of irony. I don't know if any of us have ever seen him when he's really serious" (see line 217A). Socrates, he says, is just like a Silenus statue, a surface of conventional ignorance and erotic confusion hiding a sober and temperate master, or God, within it. And what sort of mastery does this God have at his disposal? The ironic duality of everything Socrates says and does mirrors the human condition as understood by philosophy. Trapped between the finite and the infinite, the temporal and the impermanent, the incomplete and complete, in short the apparent and the real, human persons naturally strive to be rendered whole. Eros, passionate desire, is, for Socrates, the name of such striving. To understand Socrates' irony is to see his duality as exhibiting, as a lesson to us all, these facts about him. Within the world of the *Symposium*, to become ironic is to seek to emulate Socrates to become a student of his mastery.

What happens when one truly becomes Socrates' student? This is a question Plato must have pondered for a long dark time, and in the *Symposium* we find one of the answers he seems to have been most taken with. To serve Socrates, to engage properly his questions, is to work at helping to give birth to beauty seen as exemplifying an infinite, permanent, complete Good; it is to forsake appearance for Reality, to overcome uncertainty through union with Reality. It is to believe without irony in such Goods, and to allow the Ideal that such Goods exemplify to master us, to master our incomplete loves, and even our irony itself. To master the Truth is to allow it to master us. So understood, the irony with which Socrates teaches serves a mediating function. Through mediate irony, writes Alan Wilde (1981), we find a ". . .world lapsed from a recoverable norm" (p. 30). We glimpse, either through induction, reason, or imagination, a standard of perfection that not only takes us to the heart of objective goodness and truth, but provides something of a utilizable yardstick for judging our failed actuality and pointing us towards a better, "Truer," "more Real" state.

Plato, who first (in the West, at least) formulates the parameters and pedagogical value of mediate irony, is already aware of its limitations and danger. This is true even if he is ultimately correct that the spirit of Socrates is hostile to skeptical and cynical thought. It is no accident that cynics and skeptics, then and now, see *something* of their views residing in him. Even Plato, in the *Symposium* is able to wax ironically about Socratic mediate irony! In this regard Martha Nussbaum (1986), in a brilliant piece on the *Symposium*, has already argued persuasively that something more substantial lies behind the conventional comedy of Alcibiades' entrance, and encomium to Socrates. She finds there a tragic Alcibiades, someone who provides the reader with good reason to wonder about a view of love and friendship that renders concrete persons merely a means to an end, even an end as remarkable as vision of "the Good." But beyond this, I would suggest that Alcibiades' complaints are compelling to us because we find it harder and harder, in the light of a cultural experience shaped by thinkers such as Dewey and Wittgenstein, to any longer practice philosophy in the traditional manner, to viably imagine or conceive of Plato's idyllic Good or Beauty. Whether or not we prefer, in a disinterested theoretical way, a friendship guided by the Platonic ascent or a fragile love of contingent particulars is thus beside the point for our concern with irony. At least part of the poignancy we find in reading Alcibiades' encomium of Socrates stems from our fear that we are stuck with fragility, and that fragility and contingency, without a foundation in the ideal, seems in the end to yield a lightness, a nihilism, devoid of all value and purpose. In the philosophical vision of Plato, the human predicament is that of a creature suspended between appearance and reality. It is to Plato's credit that, in the character of Alcibiades, he is able, well before the onset of postmodernism and its opponents, to portray the true horror of an anxious being who loves the idea of Philosophical reality while believing in and knowing only appearance. A kind of unlucky and tragic Yahoo.

IV

One of the values of Milan Kundera's work, especially *The Unbearable Lightness of Being* (1987), is found in the way it comprehends and elaborates such fears.[6] In reading this work we discover a place in time in which nihilism becomes a real possibility, a place in time in which ideals are reduced, in the supposed absence of an "Ideal," to what Kundera calls kitsch. Our fear is that such a place and time is ours, that the book's characters exhaust enlightened human possibility. To examine some of the themes of this book is to uncover an irony that risks, in the absence of its mediation by the Ideal, by some constraint upon modern anxiety, sure emptiness and dread. In the character of Sabina, I want to suggest, Kundera provides us with a life of untethered, relentless irony that exhibits with an awful clarity what is at stake in the debate between Rorty on the one hand and the Wolins and Blooms of the world, on the other. I have already referred to the way in which Francois Ricard characterizes Kundera's irony as satanic, as a mode of radical demystification that leaves behind nothing but "...the eternal and derisory empire of accident and error." Kundera's novels, he says, "...aim to destroy the last ramparts of innocence." Beyond innocence they reveal:

> ...uncertainty, approximation, disparity, play, parody, the incongruity between the body and the soul, or between words and things, masquerade, error—in a word: Satan, God's double, but as in a mirror, a reverse double, degraded, false, ironic, absurd; a double trying to pass for the model, who succeeds more often than not, and for that reason never stops his mocking. (Ricard, 1987, p. 63)

In a somewhat similar vein Terry Eagleton (1987) refers to Kundera's unique manner of avoiding and exploding the "authoritarianism of the closed book," the "...totalitarianism of literary fiction" (p. 26). The stories Kundera tells, Eagleton claims, each have their own sense, perspective, truth. They are laid out in Kundera's novels in such a way as to defeat any reader who hopes, in Eagleton's words, to "totalize Kundera's discourse," to find overarching meaning or truth concerning events described, a way to view the novel as the world from some absolute, Philosophical perspective. Eagleton argues that because no such perspective is attainable or acceptable within the world of Kundera's novels, all events within them must appear unbearably light, accidental, contingent in the most ferocious manner possible.

There are at least several ways of understanding this refusal of innocence, this lightness Ricard and Eagleton refer to. One way, which I discuss in this section, is embodied in Kundera's character, Sabina. To refuse innocence as Sabina does is to embrace something like nihilism. Sabina, understood in this way, provides us with a perfect demonic double for the Platonic Socrates. But I will suggest in the next section that there is another way to embody lightness, a way exhibited in much of the work and life of William James. In my next section I want to begin to suggest how this *Jamesian* lightness, with its accompanying irony, provides us with a way beyond the polarity of "metaphysics or nihilism" presented so far.

Sabina is a painter, a lover of men like Franz and Tomas, and the master of betrayal. She sees her paintings, as well as social roles and institutions, just as she sees reality, as surfaces that exhibit intelligible lies, lies that hide beneath them unintelligible truths. Thus, for Sabina, all explanations, all generality, all that aims at rendering life intelligible, valuable, orderly are deceptive. A code of integrity as all-pervasive as that of Socrates forces her to treat the episodes in her life as Kundera treats the stories in his books. She refuses, as Socrates does, to allow herself to be captured in any person's or group's view of her or of her world. Thus, she is a master of betrayal. She is the ultimate enemy of kitsch, of popular taste and ugliness.

Recently much has been made of "kitsch," and Kundera's use of the term in his novel (see, for example, Greene, 1988, pp. 10, 13, 15). For Sabina, any attempt to find necessity, to uncover essential connections in the world, and to live in accordance with that necessity is kitsch, a kind of unreflective commitment to Truth, Goodness, and Certainty. Characters like Franz and Tereza and even Tomas, at one point in *The Unbearable Lightness of Being* described as the least kitsch-ridden person Sabina knows, eventually succumb in the novel to the idea that some things "must be." Sabina refuses to be ruled by such notions, even while she recognizes that kitsch cannot be totally avoided. The very act of living seems to force us to give an account of ourselves, to compose a story of our lives that implies that we are the sorts of creatures that have essences. Sabina accepts this onus of composition, but rejects the need for ultimate intelligibility. In this regard it is tempting to read Sabina as the ultimate anti-Philosopher. In her world no ultimate Philosophical sense can be made of things and every attempt to "totalize" such a sense ideal must, according to Sabina, be denied.

What is left, then, when Sabina's denials, her betrayals, cancel out the assertions of those she encounters? In Plato's Socrates the dialectic of the finite and infinite, the particular and the general, appearance and reality is reconciled in the vision and quest of perfection. But the unintelligible truth for Sabina, it seems, is that no Truth exists, except perhaps, this one enigmatic truth! Socrates' questions, at least in Plato, seem to cut through appearances to the ultimate heaviness of necessity, ultimate explanations, justifications, and essences. But at the end of Sabina's betrayals we find only the unbearable lightness of being: "...she composed a will in which she wished her dead body to be cremated and its ashes thrown to the winds....she wanted to die under the sign of lightness, she would be lighter than air" (Kundera, 1987,

p. 273). The perfection of *Saint* Sabina, as the hero of Kundera's novel, approaches that of a perfect nihilism. Sabina, understood in this way, functions as the perfect satanic double of the Socrates of the *Symposium*, another "maniac of eros," lured towards perfection as she imagines it to be. To compare Sabina to a paradigmatic teacher like Socrates as I am so far intending to do, reveals a world of horror mirroring, and at the same parodying, Plato's ironic hero.

The parallels between the way Plato portrays Socrates in the *Symposium* and the way Kundera portrays Sabina in *The Unbearable Lightness of Being* are striking. Just as Plato in the *Symposium* follows his most explicit rendering of Socrates' life and mission with Alcibiades' withering attack, Kundera follows his most explicit elucidation of Sabina's relentless rejection of kitsch in part VI of his novel with his portrayal, in part VII, of Tomas' and Tereza's idyllic married country life. Within the work of the *Symposium* Alcibiades' critique ultimately fails. Even he, who has been brought so low by Socrates, acknowledges, in a poignant moment, how the Socratic ideal forces him to hate his life pandering to the mob. As long as the reader of the *Symposium* correctly recognizes Socrates as the book's hero, such a moment must be recognized as one of truth. In a similar way the reader who takes Sabina's vision of perfect integrity as philosophically absolute can only view Tomas' and Tereza's return to marital paradise as kitsch. In the context of the novel or of Kundera's vision of the novel, should we do so?

I want to suggest that viewed from within her novelistic world Sabina's irony is nihilistic because it is, ironically, Philosophically absolute; and because it is Philosophically absolute it is, I believe, inadequate. One who takes Sabina's nihilism too seriously, too Philosophically (that is, nonironically), is faced with a number of dangers, philosophical and otherwise. What, for instance, is the status of Sabina's recognition of things? Is her rejection of all necessity, all heaviness, all explanation and universality meant to be taken seriously as capturing the essence of things, as providing the one true account of things? Are all transcendent and eternal metanarratives, all Philosophical visions corrupt *except the one that states this awareness*? Are all truths misleading *except this one*? Ricard's reading of Kundera's irony seems to make him, like his character Sabina, into a philosophical nihilist who tethers irony to simply one more philosophically questionable ideal. As a demonic double of Socrates, Sabina's philosophy has problems just as basic as that of Plato's Socrates. If we cannot believe in "The Good" because we cannot any longer believe in Philosophy, we also cannot believe in "The Void" or "The Bad" or some such thing. Sabina's pictures, like Platonic transcendental metanarratives, distinguish "reality," the intelligible "truth" from "appearance." Any irony that is to avoid the evils of Philosophical irony must transcend Plato's Socrates *and* Kundera's Sabina. Appearances *and* reality must be left behind. Both the quest for certainty for absolute truth and value, as well as the unrestrained celebration of mere chance and change, must be abandoned for a better middle ground.

Kundera (1988), in *The Art of the Novel*, says that ". . .Irony irritates. Not because it mocks or attacks but because it denies us our certainties by unmasking the world as an ambiguity" (p. 134). Read uncritically, this passage might be taken to imply that Kundera, in rejecting philosophical theory in favor of the narrative form, believes he has discovered an important, essential truth about the essential ambiguity of the human condition. Kundera, read this way, is just another confused Philosophical type in search of essential truths even as he denies the existence of essences. Read as Philosophy, Kundera's eloquent defense of the tradition of European individualism, of the novel, against philosophy sounds simply like more kitsch. If Kundera's irony is identical with Sabina's, it can be of as little value in a postmodern age as hers is.

In the remainder of this chapter I want to suggest, with the help of a line of argument implied in the work of James and Rorty, how one can have beliefs and values without a Philosophy, and, correlatively, how irony unencumbered by Philosophical ideals can nonetheless avoid nihilism, can eloquently function in defense of values of educational importance. To do this we need to resist the urge to identify Kundera with his character, Sabina. Yet I have no doubt that the novelist would sympathize with his character's refusal to take the easy route of living in certainty, of avoiding Cartesian anxiety though either a metaphysics of the Good, of idyllic nature, or of the totalitarian state. Kundera, as Rorty portrays him in works like his essay "Heidegger, Kundera, Dickens," is valuable because he exemplifies the sort of post-philosophical, postmodern perspective that allows for an irony beyond metaphysics and nihilism. According to Rorty, Kundera himself is the hero of the novels he writes because he remains ironic, rejects this false dichotomy between metaphysics and nihilism and, thus, exhibits a new possibility for irony in our time.

V

In sections III and IV I have examined, in Socrates and Sabina, two types of ironist. Neither, it seems to me, can serve as a good paradigm for the sort of person a pragmatist would care to consider well educated, a good teacher educator, or good teacher of virtue. To examine the irony of the Platonic Socrates and Kundera's Saint Sabina is to begin to both further clarify what a Rortyan ironist might ideally look like, and to begin to respond to those objections to the very idea of such an ironist to which I referred earlier.

It seems to me that many of the critics I've mentioned in section II assume that a Rortyan ironist must resemble the portrait of Sabina sketched in section IV. In fact, Allan Bloom's (1987) "cheerful nihilist" *does*, in his rejection of value, heaviness, resemble Sabina to some extent. For Bloom, products of our contemporary system of education are, however, in even worse shape than Sabina. They are nihilists who are, unlike Sabina, either too stupid or too immoral to recognize the horrible ramifications of their rejection of value and meaning. Bloom finds the cause of this deplorable situation in the pragmatic rejection of philosophy exemplified in Nietzsche, which he believes now especially dominates the higher educational establishment where most teachers are prepared.

But Sabina is certainly not a pragmatist. If my earlier sketch is correct, she is as much a Platonist, a Philosopher, in Rorty's terms as Plato's Socrates is. Like this Socrates, she has a view about the ultimate nature of Reality. As opposed to Plato's world where generality is the most Real, Sabina's "planet of inexperience" is a world where nothing repeats, where everything is its one time only, contingent particularistic self and nothing more. In this world we can never learn from our past for every case is *absolutely* unique. It would be pointless to seek rules, laws, and principles in such a world. In terms of Shulman and Sockett's shared example discussed by Pendlebury, it would be as if every golf course and every classroom were so contextually unique in time, place, and participants that absolutely no universal principles, however temporary and restricted, could be drawn.

The pragmatist is neither a universalist committed to necessary laws or particularist committed to contingent circumstances. Pragmatists, like Wittgenstein or James or Dewey, at times make use of a particularist vocabulary in order to indicate deficiencies in the universalist position; but he ought, as I understand it, to do the reverse with the particularist in need of similar therapy. The pragmatist, as I understand him or her, wants to transcend the urge, the set of questions and answers, characteristic of those engaged in the perennial debates between realists and particularists, the urge to uncover the eternal essence of things in some transcendental fixed realm.

In order to make this clearer, and to provide some material for responses to other criticisms of pragmatic ironists, I turn to a distinction

Rorty (1989) makes, in the preface to *The Consequences of Pragmatism*, between *Philosophy* and *philosophy* (pp. xiv). According to Rorty both the realist and nominalist are Philosophers. They seek the Truth, the nature of Goodness, the Real, *behind* appearances; thus, they ask questions to which both realism and nominalism are meant to provide legitimate answers. While pragmatists are never Philosophers, they may be, according to Rorty (1989), philosophers, i.e., willing to engage in attempts to "...see how things, in the broadest possible sense of the term, hang together, in the broadest possible sense of the term" (pp. xiv ff).

William James understood the value of theoretical abstraction, just as he understood the value of making distinctions. But what he worried about was the abstract reification of socially constructed theory, of the Philosophical (in Rorty's sense). Frank Lentricchia (1988) describes James's condemnation of the passionate desire (eros) for theory that amounts to "...the totalitarian site of imposition where all local situations are coerced into conformity, and where the future itself (in the form of consequences) is known and therefore controlled and manipulated in advance" (p. 107). In many ways this is precisely the effect of a great deal of educational theory and research done *on* teachers and to the results of which teachers will be held accountable by policymakers and principals. According to Lentricchia, the urge to theory in this sense leads to colonialism in politics as well as in forms of critical inquiry. Such an urge, left untempered, leads to the sorts of situations, recognized all too well in this century, where totalitarian or imperialistic regimes destroy so much of life in the name of this or that abstracted idea. It leads, in the intellectual realm, to the sort of colonialism in which one vocabulary is taken against all others, as so True to the Real as to make all difference seem merely apparent and thus, unimportant.

The pragmatic ironist need not be the sort of unengaged aesthete which critics like Wolin (1990) and Quirk (1991) believe the pragmatic ironist must be. For one can have beliefs, even philosophical, though not Philosophical, beliefs which one holds with some passion. One need not be a relativist for one can, as a consequence of reflecting on past practice, hold that some values are better, in concrete practice, than others. The pragmatic ironist can even provide reasons for believing as one does.

For the pragmatist Philosophical argument about ultimate beliefs and values has proven, over the last 2,000 years, to go nowhere but within the context of localized problems and practices all sorts of arguments, including philosophical arguments, are possible.

The pragmatic ironist, moreover, need not be a skeptic in the epistemological sense of the word. For such skepticism about the existence, say, of an external world or other minds, is a Philosophical position. The pragmatic ironist neither believes nor disbelieves, in a Philosophical sense, in such things. The pragmatic ironist takes neither the skeptic or the dichotomous cohort, the dogmatist, seriously. One simply believes in the existence of all the things and persons is justified, within the context of practice, in believing in.

Can a pragmatic ironist belong to a political community? Writers such as Alasdair MacIntyre (1981) and Michael Sandel (1982) have suggested that liberal communities, even non-ironic ones, lack the commonality of shared beliefs, passions, and practices necessary for true community. They fear that members of the liberal communities will suffer from anomie, that is, the social and personal alienation resulting from a breakdown of standards and values, that must surely characterize the sort of extreme irony practiced by the pragmatic ironist. I can imagine such critics suggesting that even the rather limited shared moral and religious commitment espoused by Dewey is impossible once we turn the pragmatist into a pragmatic ironist. In concluding this section I want to try to respond to this powerful objection.

Comments made by theologian George Linbeck (1984) in his book *The Nature of Doctrine* are relevant here. Linbeck asks questions about the status of the faith of a religious believer once such faith is formulated into theological doctrines, moral codes, or creeds. He criticizes several models of what belief in such doctrines or creeds amount to, including views of doctrine as simply propositions assented to, or as distillations of a community's experience, or the divine. His cultural linguistic model suggests that we view doctrines as offering accounts of the grammar of the practices of believers, a practice embodied in thought and action. I want to suggest that we view the religious, as well as political doctrines of the pragmatists living within an educational community, in the same light. In this way belief can be fervent, tolerant, yet leery of all theoretical, Philosophical distillations of "the one true faith."

Ironists of the sort I am describing might even share attitudes that go beyond these political commitments. In this context I mean to suggest a way that irony itself, understood as embodying an understanding of doctrines inherent in Linbeck's work, might imply a kind of respect and adherence to at least some attitudes traditionally seen as fundamental to religion. In the gospel of John, the writings of Buber on Hasidism, or in Zen mysticism one finds a kind of socio-comedy that takes up the questions dogmatically answered in traditional religious creed and metaphysical theory in order to subject them to irony. The humility and awe thus engendered for what has been called "the miracle and mystery of existence" represents a religiosity which, Jamesian fashion, "experience" replaces dogma at center stage. But "experience" is not taken here to imply mere subjectivity in the Philosophical sense. Rather it means what it did for James and Dewey, a kind of lived practice within some particular human community, for instance, the educational community.[7]

The ironist, then, as I understand, may have deep-seated political, religious, and educational commitments. But the ironist takes these commitments with a certain lightness. In other words the ironist resists all attempts to understand the doctrines one holds as immutable principles or rules. The ironist so resists the temptation to attempt the quest for certainty because one fears, as James did, the possibility that we might get stuck in the morass of traditional Philosophy with its unchanging beliefs and values. The ironist fears that such philosophizing might cause us to lose our Jamesian sense of reality, both political and religious, as too mysterious to be codified within some Philosophical theory, some final edition of the universe.

In the realm of religion, the pragmatic ironist recognizes the need for doctrines as disciplines. The pragmatic ironist knows the value of such discipline for entering more fully into the mysteries of existence, and recognizes that such disciplines cannot be practiced alone. But the irony helps one avoid ever mistaking the *discipline as vehicle* for *the end* of religious practice. The ironist recognizes that God is more, and other than the metaphors any of us use to describe a supreme mode of being, just as (to speak of the political realm) humankind is something other than the doctrines which traditional political philosophers find in various political communities.

Finally, suggestions that Rorty's pragmatic irony must be nihilistic fail to grasp what nihilism amounts to. For Nietzsche, nihilism was not simply a skepticism or relativism or aesthetic detachment concerning value.[8] It would only be nihilistic for those who believe that values can be justified only if philosophy, in Rorty's sense, is possible, i.e., if philosophical justification of some absolute value or other is possible. Once we give up on the quest for certainty and begin to look for other means of commitment and justification, it may be possible to avoid nihilism as well as skepticism, relativism, and aestheticism. In this section I have tried to show how such a case, a case for a life of non-nihilistic irony, might be made. In my next, and last substantive section, I will elaborate further. To do this I return to Kundera, and specifically to Rorty's separation of the novelist from his creation in order to imagine more carefully the parameters of the sort of pragmatic ironic community I am in the process of constructing and defending.

VI

One way to understand how the pragmatic ironist differs from, say, an aesthete-nihilist like Sabina is to discern the difference between Sabina and her creator, Milan Kundera. In a paper I mentioned earlier entitled "Heidegger, Kundera, Dickens," Rorty (1991) attempts to elaborate this difference; in so doing he provides an interpretation of Kundera as a proponent of a third way of being, beyond the lightness of a Sabina and heaviness of a Plato. There Rorty contrasts the novelist, represented by writers like Dickens, Rablais and Flaubert, as well as Kundera, with the philosopher or better (given our earlier distinction) the Philosopher. An ideally pragmatic liberal culture will cultivate and revere the novelist; it will, however, take the Philosopher much less seriously, whether he comes in the guise of a religious oracle, scientist, or pseudo-statesman.

In this article Philosophers are characterized as the ascetic priests of our civilization, as priests who strive to attain a simplicity and clarity of vision beyond mere contingency, in order to attain a vision of "the whole Other." In his characterization Rorty describes the way such Philosophers, in their flight to Being or Truth, tend always to overlook the pains and concerns of ordinary men and women. Thus, Rorty notes, it was possible for Heidegger to "...blur the distinction between automobile factories and death camps...," for Stalin to kill thousands of persons in the face of his Philosophical vision of some world-historical Marxist drama. Ascetic priests, Rorty (1991) notes, "...have no patience with people who think that mere happiness or mere decrease of suffering might compensate for *Seinsvergessenheit*, forgetfulness of being" (p. 72).

As suggested in section II, I prefer William James to Milan Kundera as the prototypical intellectual of our society. James seems to me to be clearer than the eastern European Kundera about the liberal, democratic "underpinnings" of such a society. While Kundera's books exhibit a pathos linked perhaps to an overengagement with anti-democratic writers like Nietzsche (and Heidegger), James's ethos is profoundly democratic. Whereas even the most enlightened of Kundera's characters, characters like Sabina, flirt with despair, James is relentlessly melior-istic and hopeful. Whereas Kundera at times makes his ideal characters into Philosophical particularists worshipping "absolute" contingency, James's dialectic between a concern for the individual and the whole, a dialectic further developed by Dewey, helps him avoid both solipsism and cynicism.

Moreover, reference to James rather than Kundera, allows me to acknowledge the importance of philosophy, as well as literature, to the society the pragmatist strives to attain. The philosophical attempt to see how our practices hang together, as well as how our practices might conflict or hang together with other practices, real or imagined, is surely important. Philosophers like Dewey and James, as well as traditional types like Plato, Newton, or Darwin, are valuable when they present us with visions of possible integrity or with worries about disunion. The danger, of course, is that the philosophers will stray into the quest for certainty and, thus, possibly cause us to forget the primacy of the local and practical.

VII

This chapter is intended as a start to further work in the philosophy of education of the sort just described. Critics whom I mentioned earlier have given many the impression that irony cannot provide us with a viable aim of higher education. The purpose of this chapter has been to call those very criticisms into question, to help us imagine an ironist beyond Philosophy, but not necessarily beyond philosophy, and an ironist, who unlike Plato's Socrates or Kundera's Sabina might serve as a viable prototype for a truly educated person.

In this context I have only begun to highlight a vision of William James and pragmatism, embodied both in his life and his philosophy. James was certainly not a perfect human being; perfection, in any event, is in the end a term ultimately for Philosophers. Yet his instincts, both as far as philosophy and culture, were, I believe, healthy ones, ones worth examining and emulating.

In again reading James over the last few months I have discovered a vision much more admirable than one finds in the typically fashionable caricature of his work. Here is no crude philosophy of commercialism; no careful reading of James's (1936) critique, in *The Varieties of Religious Experience*, of "healthy mindedness" could accuse him of reducing the Western philosophical tradition to happy cash values. One can find, in James's pragmatism and radical empiricism, a critique of traditional philosophical pretensions as complete and moving, as tough minded, as anything one finds in Heidegger, or Nietzsche. And in James's work one can begin to see how such a "postmodern" point of view is consistent with a militantly democratic commitment to difference as well as dialogue within the community.

In the initial lecture of *Pragmatism* James (1981) speaks of two worlds, the world of, in Rorty's sense, Philosophy and the world of ordinary practice. He worries about the sort of philosophy that becomes the search for fixed and final eternal principles, a "marble temple shining on a hill," a simple, clean, noble world within the contradictions of everyday life." While he is aware that such theories may, in various contexts, have their use, he fears that all too often these edifices become substitutes for everyday lived practice, remedies, ways of escape.

In a later lecture, James (1981), whether happily or not, speaks of pragmatism as a woman who might unstiffen the theories which Philosophers provide us with (p. 9). In short, pragmatism might show us how to turn Philosophy into philosophy, how to make the urge to theory useful to, rather than an escape from, life. In this regard much of the work of John Dewey, James's disciple, can be seen as embodying a search for further agents of unstiffening. James, like Dewey, dreamed of a time when philosophy might reject its fantasy quest for pure theory, for certainty, and might return to engage real problems of human beings in their search for security and happiness.

In too-often-ignored essays such as "The Sentiment of Rationality" and "The Moral Philosopher and the Moral Life," James (1956) makes it clear where such a lived world of practice can be found. While "reason vs. emotion" is ideally a dichotomy best left those that seek ultimate theoretical explanation, James, in his historical context, rightly prefers desire to reason as the locus of the real. Desire, not thought, lies at the center of James's philosophy. No philosopher (the small *p* is doubly intended here), not even Wittgenstein, does a better job than James of revealing the sterility of pure thought divorced from contingent and mutual desires of everyday practice.

To make sense of James's pragmatic irony will require that we explore the contours of his world of passionate desire. For this world, a world of intelligent thought to be sure, but not transcendental Reason, a world less grandiose but more honest than some philosophical mansion on the hill, is the world where we live and breathe, hope and despair, plot and feel. It is a world, I want to claim, in which irony, ironically enough, has a legitimate claim to attention. It is a world of scientists with lab rats inside laboratories, bureaucrats and citizens inside public buildings, and micro-accountable teachers with students inside classrooms.

CHAPTER 6

Emptiness

_____ *Leonard J. Waks*

Each of the world's great civilizations has been influenced profoundly by intellectual and ethical teachers identified as "paradigmatic" individuals by the philosopher Karl Jaspers (1962). They attained, and attempted to teach, an experience of wholeness—the intimate embrace of all reality and oneness with all people. They learned to face bitter truths about the world and human life without flinching. By overcoming their fears, inhibitions, and obsessions, they were able to grasp intuitively, and express clearly, those deep truths which even simple and inarticulate people long to understand. They were at once profound seers, gentle teachers of moral values, and simple friends of humanity.

Socrates, Jesus, and Gautama the Buddha are such paradigmatic teachers. They attained mythic status as masters and teachers of the art of living. The personal obstacles they encountered in obtaining and sharing their wisdom and insight are widely known; the stories of their lives, discoveries, and teachings are told in the greatest books of all time.

Institutions devoted to keeping these wisdoms and their discoveries alive and teaching them to humanity anew have often occasioned experiences of separateness and isolation. Their polar thinking has at times reduced unifying insights to slogans of separate warring camps. Contemporary teachers embracing "whole person" and "one world" perspectives walk in the footsteps of these great teachers—they long to experience, and to share, that sense of wholeness and unity in our fragmented and divided world.

We can see the contemporary relevance of these great teachers by appreciating the unifying and trans-cultural, rather than the culturally specific, themes in their ideas. In this chapter I consider three ideas: Socratic ignorance, Christian poverty, and Buddhist emptiness. Despite different cultural frameworks of ideas and practices, these ideas share a penetrating insight regarding conditions for the experience of unity and wholeness.

Socratic Ignorance

Understanding Socratic ignorance will require some preliminaries about Socrates' divine mission and his understanding of the soul. In Plato's *Apology* (Tredennick, 1959) Socrates tells of a quest ordained for him by the gods. This mission compels him to probe with his fellow Athenians the bases of their life-directing values, and to encourage them to seek the nature of the good and the best way of living. The project made him abandon other life goals, and proclaim that "wealth does not bring goodness, but goodness brings wealth and every other blessing..." (Tredennick, 1959, p. 62).

Socrates must not have meant wealth in the ordinary, monetary sense, but rather that which truly enriches human life. His way of living left him in poverty, and exposed to the barbs of the comic poets. Amipsias joked that Socrates had been "born to spite the shoemakers," and Eupolis called Socrates a "garrulous beggar, who has ideas about everything except how to get a meal" (Burnett, 1968, p. 132). Despite this ridicule, his probing stung many of his fellow Athenians; they accused Socrates of corrupting the youth of the city, and placed him on trial for his life.

Instead of apologizing and begging the jury to spare him, Socrates provoked them with yet another discomforting philosophy lesson. He asserted that his fellow citizens might indeed destroy his body. But something far more valuable, something at the very core of a life worth living, would be destroyed if, out of fear, he were to abandon the guiding principles of his life. This more valuable something he called his "psyche" or soul (see chapter 7), and scholars credit Socrates with the original discovery that the life-directing principles which recommend themselves to conscious reasoning are the core of the "psyche."

To understand Socrates' insight, it is useful to consider the understanding of the "psyche" before Socrates. Earlier Greeks had a primitive explanation for the mystery of life—they posited the presence of a ghost-like double entering the body at birth and departing at death. For example, a person might be admonished to "care for his soul"—to keep the psyche from departing, i.e., to be cautious, to protect one's life from danger. But fifth century Greeks, says Burnett, were not likely to take the idea of a ghost-like animating spirit either seriously or literally. Nonetheless, there remained some weak associations with the idea of the double in fifth century literary uses, and Burnett explores two which are relevant; the connection of "psyche" with waywardness and conscience.

People in Athens were no less troubled by inexplicable feelings and appetites than we are in our self-conscious age. But instead of accepting such wayward emotions as parts of themselves, they spoke of them, perhaps half seriously, as belonging to these doubles, their psyches. In this usage, to care for one's psyche meant to provide for its wayward needs. Thus, Cyclops in Euripides's *Cyclops* thinks that by eating Odysseus he will be doing his psyche a good turn (Burnett, 1968, p. 155). One cares for the psyche, as one "feeds the animal within," by taking a moral holiday.

But such waywardness may lead to a troubled conscience. In the *Republic*, even the placid Cephalus is awakened at night with the guilty dreams of his psyche. In his thinking it is not his waking self whose wrong doing causes guilt feelings, but its double, the shadow-like psyche which awakens when the waking self sleeps. The psyche's guilty dream awakens Cephalus much as might the loud snoring of his wife.

Socrates broke away from such remnants of double-think, conceiving of the psyche as simply the everyday self, the directing ego. For him, the psyche was the organ for the rational care and management of one's life. Caring for the soul, in the Socratic sense, thus meant striving for those excellences of character which protected and promoted one's best life. And to damage the soul in this sense was to ruin those capacities by virtue of which one might live well. While one might live an acceptable life after losing an arm or leg, one could only live an undirected, broken, pitiful, and altogether lost life with a ruined soul. Clearly, such a life could not be worth living.

By reclaiming wayward desires and guilt for the directing ego, Socrates offered his listeners a path to psychic wholeness. Of course, he knew, they could not rationally and self-consciously will evil (see chapter 7). But by owning up to wayward thoughts and bad intentions, by taking full responsibility for them, they could subject them to rational re-evaluation. And by a rational redirection of will, they then could turn away from them toward the good.

However, rational inquiry into the good raises the problem of moral knowledge, and leads to consideration of Socratic ignorance. Even as a young man Socrates was thought unusually wise (Burnett, 1968, p. 133). It is this that led Charerophon to ask the Delphic Oracle if anyone were wiser, and when the oracle answered in the negative, Socrates set out to verify this for himself. He interviewed those most esteemed for their wisdom, and discovered that they were really not wise. Instead, they were frequently closed to fresh insight because they thought they knew many things about which they were actually ignorant. He concluded that the oracle was correct, in a paradoxical way; no one was wiser than he, because while he was, like the others, quite ignorant, he could accept his ignorance. The others had too much to live up to; they were too frightened or proud to face their ignorance, and their defensive barriers stood in the way of new insight.

Through dialogical encounters, Socrates picked away at the definitions and arguments of the citizens of Athens, attempting to open their minds to life-transforming insight. He reveled in his ignorance, denying that he had any speculative opinions to defend. He proclaimed human knowledge and wisdom to be of no worth whatsoever, compared to the gods (Tredennick, 1959, p. 52).

This skepticism about human knowledge led him to what could be called a "heroic fallibilist voluntarist" ethic. Ignorance is universal, and because people can never *know* the good with finality (fallibilism), they are never done with searching the ground of their obligations and the logical implications of their free choices. Using a military analogy, he said that people must, without a sufficient rational basis, "take up their stand in life" (voluntarism), and "there they are bound to remain and face the danger, taking no account of death or anything else before dishonor" (heroism) (Tredennick, 1959, p. 60).

Those who "desert their post" without good and sufficient reason deserve public trial and condemnation. Only logical reasons, not personal risks, should move a person from his chosen "stand." People should take no advice, even from the closest friends, "unless reflexion shows it to be the best course that reason offers." But we also must be ready to abandon our old principles when by reasoned inquiry we "can find better principles to guide us..." (Tredennick, 1959, p. 84). To act otherwise is to ruin "the part of us...in which right and wrong operates," the organ which is "mutilated by wrong actions..." (p. 86), to lose the capacity for rational self-direction, our best habits, the content of our character. With that gone we are lost souls, and our lives can no longer be worth living.

The life which this kind of reasoning recommended to Socrates consisted of investigating with his proud fellow Athenians the grounds for their actions and their lives. By exposing the irrational foundations of their lives, he was on his view doing for them the best thing that could possibly be done. He was "caring for" and even "salvaging" their souls.

In the *Republic* Plato revisited the Socratic mission in the familiar analogy of ascent from the dark cave. Each stage in liberation from the cave is fraught with pain and suffering, because comforting delusions are destroyed long before more adequate ideas can form. The passage from the cave to the outer world, representing the beginning of rational awareness, is depicted as the most distressing. The "light of day" destroys cave thinking long before anything can be grasped of the new reality, and the liberated person is entirely disoriented and confused. A period of adjustment is needed before the real world can be apprehended and understood for what it is.

But this final experience of the real, of the One, is for the Platonic Socrates at one and the same time a direct perception of the Good, the source of all virtue. And this is also the most beautiful of all ideas to contemplate. But because those who have directly apprehended the Good are themselves good, they are just and seek the good not just for themselves, but for all others. Despite their love of the One, they are willing to return, with their wisdom, to free the pitiful dwellers of the cave.

Christian Poverty

Necessary background for the Christian concept of poverty is found throughout the Hebrew Bible, but particularly in the book of *Exodus*. Yahweh, the God of the Israelites, commanded Moses to lead His people out of slavery and into the desert, that is, the empty land, in order that they might be purified and prepared to receive His law. When the Israelites were disoriented by desert life, Yahweh sent down His own bread of life, to provide sufficiently for their every need so they did not have to struggle for survival. After the purification of the desert, Yahweh gave Moses the law on Mt. Sinai in the form of ten commandments, and told the Israelites that if they obeyed these commandments, they would come to possess a rich and glorious realm.

The first and core commandment was that the Israelites were to love their God—the one and sufficient One "I Am"—and to have no other gods before Him; they were to set their sights, and place their faith, in Him alone. The other laws addressed elements of morality and rituals of worship.

On one level, this story tells of the consciousness of a people with a slave mentality. Craving security, they were terrified that left to themselves their needs will go unmet. They have no faith and cannot trust the sufficiency of being. They cannot set their sights on the One, even though He appears and speaks directly to them. Their consciousness rapidly returns to their own needs and they forget everything. Their craving for the secure and familiar is symbolized in their worship of an idol, the golden calf.

But the story also reinforces an idea expressed by Socrates: wealth and every other blessing goes to those who set the habits of their hearts on the Real and the Good. As the Platonic Socrates saw it, the One who is also the Good, is abundant and entirely sufficient. By turning entirely to the One, the all-encompassing God "I Am," by letting go of anxious clinging in favor of radical openness to reality—we are promised the most intimate possession of all riches.

This brings us to Jesus and poverty. Jesus prepared himself for his teaching by going off into the wilderness—the empty land, his own private desert—for forty days of silence and fasting. Fasting in isolation brings many inner demons out of hiding, and we are told that after this long fast Jesus was "hungry," that is, he felt needy and vulnerable. This encouraged the demon to try to snare him. He said that if the Son of God were hungry, he could make bread out of stones—that is, derive life's strength from non-life. Jesus replied that he would take his nourishment instead from every word proceeding from the mouth of the living God. Then the demon pulled out all the stops, offering Jesus a vision and promise of world domination. But Jesus emptied himself of attachment to all earthly power and glory, and could thus speak and teach for God.

His first lesson was stated in the form of a paradox: "Blessed are the poor in spirit," he said, "for theirs is the kingdom of God." The genuinely poor are destitute, they have nothing; therefore, they are open to receive the kingdom that God has promised. That kingdom is indeed theirs already. The poor are empty, and so they are blessed and lucky because unlike old wine bottles, they can right now be completely filled with new wine.

Jesus developed this explanation further by drawing an analogy in his next Beatitude with a funeral or wake. Lucky are those who suffer. Only those who actually mourn, who experience loss and emptiness, can be comforted (*Matthew* 5:3-4). Those who cannot mourn cannot be comforted and get beyond mourning.

This understanding of poverty as emptiness goes hand in hand with the kind of child-like innocence which Jesus said was needed to enter the Kingdom, "The one who makes himself as little as this little child is the greatest in the kingdom of heaven" (*Matthew* 18:4). Infants are potentialities. They do not yet have anything to live up to, so they cling to nothing, and thus nothing stands in the way of fresh insight or truth.

This paradox is also expressed by Paul (2 *Corinthians* 6: 7-10) when he says of the apostalate that: We are people who possess nothing and hence have everything. And in *Philippians* 2:5-7 Paul notes that though Jesus's state was divine, he did not cling to his equality with God, but emptied himself to assume the condition of the lowest servant. Jesus entered the Kingdom by dint of emptiness. Though rich with worldly possibilities, he laid these down like Socrates, to become poor on behalf of all others.

And like Socrates, Jesus found the so-called "teachers and wise men" of his day filled with pride about their understanding and observance of God's commandments. They made a public display of legalistic observances while clinging to rules, laws, and worldly goods. He taught in parables, which forced his listeners to think through the deeper meanings for themselves. For example, he taught that the Kingdom of Heaven is like a grain of mustard seed; it is the smallest of all seeds, but when it is grown it becomes a tree so tall that the birds of the air come and nest in its branches (*Matthew* 13:32). The greatest good is unseen amidst the baubles of life. With care, it blossoms into something great and wonderful, with great potentialities for beautiful new life within its many lofty "branches."

But Jesus knew that even such powerful analogies would gain little hold on the minds of those delighted by their old values and ideas; again by analogy, he said that no one can put new wine in old wine bottles. While unlike Socrates he did not seek directly to confront those who he thought to be taking the wrong path of life, like Socrates his teaching aroused acute discomfort and hostility, and Jesus, too, was killed.

The late thirteenth century Dominican philosopher Meister Eckhart explored Jesus's idea of poverty in his sermon on *Matthew* 5:3, "Blessed are the Poor in Spirit" (Colledge and McGinn, 1981, pp. 199–203). He noted that mere economic poverty, whatever its moral or religious value, could not bring about an experience of wholeness. He said that a person may be called "poor" in the *relevant* sense only when he *wills* nothing, *knows* nothing, and *has* nothing.

A person who *wills* or desires nothing more than to fulfill God's will still wills something, and thus is not poor. He says: before I entered the world of becoming as a creature of God, "I longed for nothing, I wanted nothing, I was an empty being," and for a man to be poor in will, he must "want or desire as little as when he did not exist" (Colledge and McGinn, 1981, p. 200).

Similarly, to be poor a person should *know* nothing—not even know God or that God lives in him, but should be "set...free of his own knowing." There is something in the human soul from which knowledge flows, which makes knowledge possible, but that something does not itself know, but merely "rejoices in itself." "Whoever will be poor in spirit, he must be poor of all his own knowledge, so that he knows nothing, not God or created things or himself" (p. 201) (compare with Socratic ignorance).

Finally, a person who *has* anything is not poor. Suppose that a person is so free of all attachments to possessions and hopes as to become only a place within which God can work. Such a person is still not in the requisite sense poor for "poverty of spirit is for a man to keep so free of God and all of his works that if God wishes to work in the soul, he himself is the place in which he wants to work" (p. 202). A person should not be or have any place for God to work, for "when a man clings to place, he clings to distinction." When God finds nothing left in a person, not even a place in which to do his work, when all distinctions dissolve, then God becomes "one with the spirit, and that is the most intimate poverty one can find" (p. 203).

Further light may be thrown on this passage by considering the sixth of Eckhart's *Counsels on Discernment* (Colledge and McGinn, 1981, pp. 247–284) where Eckhart asks us to think about the experience of a very thirsty man. Whatever he turns his mind to, he remains conscious of being thirsty. The more the thirst grows, "the more the idea of drinking grows and intrudes and possesses him," until at last he is consumed by thirst, and nothing is left of him except thirst itself (p. 253). Similarly, if a man loves something ardently and with all his heart, then wherever he is, and whatever he is doing, what he so loves never passes from his heart—he sees it in everything he encounters.

In like manner a man who loves God becomes "shaped through and through with the shape of God," becomes one with Him (p. 253). In a startling passage, which attempts to express this quality of experience, Eckhart says that it is the experience of being "one in that One where all multiplicity is one and is one unmultiplicity" (p. 252). The empty consciousness is completely *adequate* to all distinctions, while clinging to none. This awareness is clear, vibrant, dynamic, and without distortion. Everything it discriminates is also experienced as an aspect of a complete and perfect whole—a multiplicity which is one unmultiplicity.

Buddhist Emptiness

Gautama the Buddha abandoned his life of wealth, power, and delusion when he was confronted with the existential problems of living: illness, aging, and death, and saw that wealth and power offered no solutions to these problems. Initially he attempted to resolve these problems through ascetic practices, and discovered that a mere external emptiness and renunciation were also not relevant to their solution. He too was described as "hungry" after a long fast. Renouncing external and superficial emptiness, he sat under a Banyon tree (a tree, revered throughout India, whose aerial roots grow into new trunks so that it can constantly renew its life) and there accepted a bowl of milk. Thus refreshed, he sat under the Bodhi tree—the *Ficus Religiosa* or Tree of Enlightenment—and entered a meditative state in which he resolved to think through and solve once and for all the problems of life and death (Saddhatissa, 1976, p. 31).

Like Jesus, he was confronted by a demon willing to pull out all of the stops—to offer all worldly temptations—and he, too, worked his way through these to freedom and enlightenment.

When he thought about how to teach, how to share his insight, he at first despaired. But compassion brought him, like Socrates and Jesus, to search for fresh formulations and methods of teaching which could penetrate the consciousness of his listeners and stimulate their own inner processes of life-transforming thought.

He formulated his first lesson in a simple syllogism: Life is suffering. Suffering is caused by addictive craving (for wealth, pleasures, worldly importance, prestige, speculative knowledge, etc.) If craving can be ended, suffering can be ended, and craving *can* be ended.

He saw people suffering because they were unwilling to confront the problems of living directly, insisting instead upon wasting their lives in irrational strivings for unattainable ends (e.g., sufficient power or wealth or physical beauty to avoid death) or for trivialities which merely distracted them from their problems. He shaped his teaching in the form of a set of laws (the so-called eight-fold noble path) for entering nirvana, an experiential condition of wholeness and completeness which signified the ultimate defeat of the problem of aging and death.

The initial step on this path is "right understanding," grasping the fundamental precept that craving is the cause of suffering. In a sense, this is also the final step, for all other steps exist primarily to deepen this understanding. The intermediate steps emphasize living simply and harmlessly.

The final step involves "right meditation," eventuating in a deep state of empty-mindedness. As Johansson (1969) states, the immediate purpose of this mental state is to reduce the amount of conscious contents until the mind is completely motionless and empty. This is a state of samadhi, emptiness of consciousness, and may be thought of as an emptiness of the mind's *surface*.

However, the process of growth along the Buddhist path demands more than a superficially *empty* mind; rather, it demands an altogether clear mind, within which the last vestiges of compulsive sensuality and willful ignorance may be faced rationally and squarely. Only when all traces of the addictive cravings have been eliminated by a *rational examination* of the delusions which sustain them, and the costs which they exact, can a person attain emptiness in the deepest sense, a radical emptiness of inner personality in which the root causes of cravings and ignorance have been altogether eliminated (Johansson, 1969, pp. 27, 103–109).

The experience of nirvana, the sense of unity resulting from this insight, is also called "sunyata" or emptiness. In nirvana the subjective self and its objects are experienced as empty—i.e., mere phenomena without any real, substantial existence. When this is understood, there can be no further clinging to either the experience of self or its objects; consciousness is free, undistorted, flexible, discriminating, and complete.

This idea is beautifully illustrated in another startling passage, this one from D.T. Suzuki's "Early Memories" in *The Field of Zen* (1970). When Suzuki was twenty-one he was under the instruction of Kosen Roshi, Abbot of Engakuji, and was impressed by his directness and simplicity. But one of the Roshi's lectures in particular was unforgettable.

> It was on the 42nd chapter of the *Hekiganroku*, the one where Ho-koji visits Yakusan, and after the interview Yakusan tells ten monks to see him off down the mountain to the temple gate. On the way the following conversation takes place: "Fine snow falling flake by flake, each flake falls in its own proper place."
>
> This struck me as a strange subject for Zen monks to talk about, but the Roshi just read the passage without a word of explanation, reading as though he were entranced and absorbed by the words of the text. I was so impressed by this reading, even though I did not understand a word, that I can still see him sitting in his chair with the text in front of him reading "Fine snow falling flake by flake." (p. 6)

Here in the absorption of fine snow flakes falling, each in its proper place, we find the experience, indicated by Eckhart, of reality as a multiplicity-in-process-of-becoming as One and one unmultiplicity. Reality is grasped without modification or attachment in the mind of the knower. Everything is seen as it is, here and now, without clinging or emotional distortion.

Even people's lives and predicaments can also be seen clearly. From the nirvana standpoint, even the self is a process, not a fixed substance. So bodhisattvas (Buddhist seers) can accept any feature of their own consciousness; they have no need to reject, deny, dissociate, or project any aspect of themselves. And because of this radical self-openness, they can also face and accept others. For there is nothing in others which is *fundamentally* other, nothing in others which they might not experience in themselves. In their humanness, they and others are one. Thus, emptiness is the standpoint not merely for profound intellectual penetration of reality, but also for compassion and unconditional love. Buddhists express this in the teaching that "maha prajna," the great wisdom, *is* "maha karuna," the great compassion (Suzuki, 1970, pp. 38–43).

This identity resonates with the Socratic identity of knowledge and goodness, and with the Platonic identity of the One and that Good by reference to which philosophers can guide the community to its highest good. In our Judeo-Christian tradition, we express this insight when we say that the God "I Am" *is* Love.

Conclusion

Socrates, Jesus, and Gautama are the paradigmatic teachers of Eastern and Western civilization. For them, preparation for teaching first necessitated emptiness, the radical openness to reality, including the often shocking reality of the human heart. This emptiness cut through the dualisms of subject/object and self/other, condemned by Dewey and made possible the unencumbered participation in the infinite intelligence and dynamic creativity that lies beyond well-bounded individual selves, at the core of being. For them, teaching meant sharing with others in that participation.

But the "march of progress" since the seventeenth century has displaced such philosophical ideas from discussions of teaching, learning, and education. The Enlightenment and the Industrial Revolution have placed the abstract rules and principles, reductive scientific studies, nature-dominating technology, and "natural law" at the center of the educational enterprise. Even the arts have taken on a quasi-scientific character as academic disciplines. Teaching and learning themselves have also been transformed; when reconceived in the favored terms of the scientific-technical culture, teaching has been reduced to technical control. The study of teaching has been dominated by reductive analyses of technical effectiveness; teacher "training" means a regime to improve technical control over others.

As the modern project collapses, it is timely to place such ideas in larger cultural perspective. Those thinking about teaching may seek to discover a larger pattern. They may wish to contrast the unifying vision of the paradigmatic teachers with these impermanent and life-diminishing myths of control and the quest for absolute certainty. In these investigations, emptiness provides the point of departure.

CHAPTER 7

Soul

Sophie Haroutunian-Gordon

The word "soul" occurs but rarely in contemporary educational discourse. How things have changed since the time of Plato, for whom talk of education had little interest except in conjunction with talk of the soul. The shift in our rhetoric may have origins in the Greek tradition itself, as the analysis here demonstrates. To begin with, the Greek word for soul, namely psyche, has a long history of alternative translation ("psyche" rather than "soul")—a history which has dominated educational discourse since the late nineteenth century.[1]

While much of educational significance has been learned from psychology, it may have inclined us away from talk of the soul, and to some disadvantage, it seems. For Plato's view of the soul offers a powerful vision of education, as many have recognized. Consider the following passage from the _Republic_, Book VII:

> Education is not in reality what some people proclaim it to be in their professions. What they aver is that they can put true knowledge into a soul that does not possess it, as if they were inserting vision into blind eyes.
>
> They do indeed.
>
> But our present argument indicates that the true analogy for this indwelling power in the soul and the instrument whereby each of us apprehends is that of an eye that could not be converted to the light except by turning the whole body. Even so this organ of knowledge must be turned around from the world of becoming together with the entire soul, like the scene-shifting periactus in the theater, until the soul is able to endure the contemplation of essence and the brightest region of being. (518 b–d)[2]

Through dialogue with Glaucon, Socrates comes to define education as leading or drawing vision out of the student rather than putting it in. And where does the vision reside—from whence is it to be drawn?

97

From the "soul" says Socrates, and to speak of education is to speak of "turning the soul."

From Augustine to Kant to Rousseau to Dewey to Montessori to A.S. Neill to Mortimer Adler, theorists have reaffirmed Plato's conviction that education is "drawing out" vision or understanding—*educare*. Even Dewey's emphasis upon constructing knowledge through inquiry was based upon drawing out the student's ideas about situations (see Haroutunian-Gordon, 1991, pp. 12-16).

Despite our philosophical roots in Plato's writings, however, educational practice in the present day (as was true in Plato's) is frequently defined around the opposite claim—that education is rather a matter of putting understanding into blind, ignorant students. Education, we often say, is a matter of *instruere* rather than *educare*—of building up or "furnishing with knowledge" (Oxford English Dictionary, 1971) rather than drawing out of students that which they believe and understand. Given the former perspective, the failure of our educational system may be said to arise from our failure to impart knowledge and skills. Our task as teachers, then, is to determine that which students should know (Hirsch, 1987) and "present it" in the most efficacious manner. Indeed, we frequently treat the failing student as if there were no vision—no understanding—to be drawn out of that ignorant soul. Today, there is precious little talk of "soul turning" with reference to such students, and much bemoaning of our failure to impart knowledge and skills.

From what source do these quite contradictory beliefs about the nature and failings of education arise? We will return to this question after some analysis. To help wend our way there, let us begin by exploring the two analogies that Plato presents in the passage from the *Republic* formerly quoted. The first is the "true analogy" for the indwelling power in the soul and the "instrument whereby each of us apprehends." The image he offers is that of a body coupled with an eye. The eye—analogous to the instrument of apprehension—can see only under a particular circumstance, namely, when the body in which it is housed turns and "looks" with it. In that instance, the power to see, which is analogous to the turning body, enables the eye to apprehend because both are directed toward the right spot.

Second, he draws an analogy between the soul with its indwelling power and instrument of apprehension and a piece of theatrical apparatus known as the *periaktoi*. According to ancient authority on the subject, Vitruvius, the periaktoi were "triangular pieces of machinery which revolve, each having three decorated faces and three kinds of scene—tragic, comic, and satyric" (Vince, 1984, p. 55). A mechanical device beneath the periaktoi would turn the triangular pieces simultaneously so that a contribution to the new scene would spread across the face of each at the same moment. The apparatus would change the scene of the play, but would do so only when the faces of all the periaktoi shifted together.

Now, not only do the eye and its body turn after the fashion of the periaktoi, but like the device, they also turn from darkness to light. The periaktoi, Vitruvius suggests, shifted so that the faces which once looked back onto the stage or off to the side now look toward the front, i.e., they face the audience. Likewise, Plato says the "organ of knowledge," analogous to the turning body, must, along with its "instrument of apprehension," "be turned around from the world of becoming, until [it] is able to endure contemplation of essence and the brightest region of being." According to Platonic metaphysics, the "world of becoming" is darkness, as no truth can be seen there. Only when the soul looks toward the world of being can the truth or essence of things be apprehended. For in that world there is light.

Many today reject talk of transcendental "being" and "essence," but let us not let problems with Plato's metaphysics spoil the beauty of his analogies and the insights that they offer into teaching and learning. Surprisingly enough, these insights seem to have their roots in a deep ambiguity that the image of the periaktoi presents. The ambiguity is this: On the one hand, the periaktoi were looked upon. In setting the scene for a piece of the drama, they would seem to be analogous to—a metaphor for—the light which allows the audience to see the play, i.e., to recognize its fundamental character as comic, tragic, or satyric. On the other hand, only when the panels of the periaktoi face the audience do they set the scene. For while they face the back of the stage or the side regions of the theater, they are dark and no one can see them, so they cannot shed light upon the meaning of the action that is taking place on stage. When they face the audience, however, the audience views them so that now they can "throw light" upon the action. But, they throw no such light until they are viewed—until the vision of the onlookers throws light upon them. So the question arises: Are we to think of the periaktoi as that which permits something else (the character of the drama) to be seen, or is it that which itself is seen?

This very point of ambiguity seems to be present in Plato's conception of the soul, at least as Socrates speaks of it at *Republic* 518 c–d. For Socrates tells us that the soul has "indwelling power," or knowledge of what is true. It provides, therefore, that which needs to be seen. At the same time, it must be "turned around from the world of becoming" until it is able to "endure contemplation of the essence"—

until it is able to tolerate contemplation of what it knows to be true. Only when the soul has been properly turned toward "the light"—toward appropriate objects—can such contemplation take place. Is the soul, or its indwelling power, to be thought of as that which is seen, or is it that which permits the seeing to take place?

In recognizing the above ambiguity in Plato's use of the term "soul," we are alerted to two other places in the educational context where this same ambiguity arises. The first concerns the role of the text, or if you will, the materials that the teacher directs the students to look upon. Is the text that which is seen or that which permits the seeing to take place? Consider the following class of students discussing Shakespeare's *Romeo and Juliet* (Haroutunian-Gordon, 1991, pp. 85–100). This group of fifteen-year-olds has finished reading the famous "balcony scene" in which Romeo and Juliet reveal their feelings of love and attraction toward one another, despite the animosity between their families. The classroom teacher, Mrs. Prince, opens with a question (pp. 91-92):

> Mrs. Prince: Well, one thing I noticed about Juliet is that she never says, "Go home." [Even though it is dangerous for Romeo to be there in Juliet's garden]...Why doesn't she tell Romeo to go away?
> Colette: Because she is in love with him.
> Sophie: So she is in love, Colette, but she knows he is in danger. Still, she doesn't tell him to leave.
> Colette: Right.
> Mrs. Prince: She wants him to be there?
> Colette: Right.
> Marcy: They love each other.
> Mrs. Prince: They love each other but she never tells him to go. Don't you think that is interesting? If you love somebody and they come to your house, and they are in danger if they stick around—may get hurt—but you never tell the person to go. Isn't that interesting? Colette.
> Colette: If she don't tell him to go she is trying to get him hurt.
> Sophie: Do you think she is trying to get him hurt? Sylvia.
> Sylvia: No, she's in love and she wants to see her man. If he leaves and gets hurt, she might never see him again.
> Marcy: I think she's trying to tell him to come over to her house.
> Sophie: So she wants him to come in, Marcy?
> Marcy: Yeah.
> Sophie: But doesn't she worry about it?

Marcy: She said, if they see him outside they are going to get him. She is trying to give him the idea to come into her bedroom.
James: She wants to hide him?
Marcy: No, she doesn't. She wants to get married.

From this exchange, it appears that the text—the scene from *Romeo and Juliet* that is under discussion—is itself the focus of study. The students and teachers ponder a question which the text seems to offer as one looks at it, namely why Juliet does not tell Romeo to leave the garden since she knows that by remaining he is in mortal danger. It appears, then, that the aim of the discussion is to make sense of the text—to see its meaning.

But is this the aim of the discussion? As they reflect upon the text, we see the students drawing out of themselves beliefs that they have about why people act as they do under certain circumstances. Why doesn't Juliet tell Romeo to leave? Because she loves him and wants him there with her, begins Colette; because she may never see him again if he leaves and gets hurt, says Sylvia; because she wants to entice him into her bedroom (not hide him), insists Marcy. This text, focusing as it does on adolescent love, draws out of these adolescent readers beliefs about the effects of love—beliefs they may never have articulated before. The text, then, seems both to illuminate those beliefs—to shed light upon them—and to itself be illuminated by them. It occupies the same ambiguous position as the periaktoi in Socrates' analogy: Is it that which is seen, or that which permits seeing to take place?

Consider finally, the relationship between the student and the teacher: Is it the teacher who sheds the light so that the students may see—who permits seeing to take place? If we consider once again the preceding example, this might seem to be the case. Here, the teacher, Mrs. Prince, poses a question: Why doesn't Juliet tell Romeo to go away—to leave the garden? In trying to answer the question, the students draw out their beliefs about the effects of love, so it would seem that the teacher, through questioning, is shedding light and allowing the students to see that which is there to be seen.

At the same time, the beliefs which the students draw out of themselves as they address the question draw out of the teachers (and other students) further questions and ideas—ones that were not present at the start of the conversation. When Marcy says that Juliet does not tell Romeo to leave because she loves him, this deepens Mrs. Prince's puzzle:

They love each other but she never tells him to go. Don't you
think that is interesting? If you love somebody, and they come
to your house, and they are in danger if they stick around—
may get hurt—but you never tell the person to go. Isn't that
interesting?

Likewise, when Marcy suggests that Juliet wants Romeo to come
into her bedroom, rather than leave the garden, James has a new
question: "She wants to hide him?"

Who is the student and who is the teacher in a conversation such
as the one above? Who sheds the light? And where are the truths—the
ideas—located upon which the light is shed? Like the periaktoi, the
position occupied by the so-called "students" and "teachers" is ambiguous: Both seem to be seen and both seem to allow the seeing to
take place. For both offer ideas that others in turn reflect upon, and
in so doing, permit others to have ideas that they had not had before.

Let us return to our opening dilemma. Socrates claims:

Education is not in reality what some people proclaim it to be
in their professions. What they aver is that they can put true
knowledge in a soul that does not possess it, as if they were
inserting vision into blind eyes.

But, if education is not inserting vision into blind eyes, why do we often
practice as though this were the case? And why do we frequently define
our failure to educate as one of failing to "furnish" the students with
knowledge or skills? The present analysis suggests a response to this
puzzling question, namely, that drawing out ideas looks very much
like putting them in, at least in some instances. When James asks Marcy
whether Juliet "wants to hide Romeo," one could say that Marcy has
"put this idea into his head" by saying that Juliet wants Romeo to come
into her bedroom. Likewise, when Sylvia says that Juliet is "in love and
wants to see her man. If he leaves and gets hurt, she might never see
him again," one might argue that Sophie "gave her" that idea by
questioning Colette's claim that Juliet was trying to "get Romeo hurt."

Since "drawing ideas out" may look very much like putting them
in, it is not so surprising that educational practice divides itself between
these two views of what it is doing. The ambiguity has its roots in Book
VII of the *Republic,* as the image of the periaktoi makes clear: That which
sheds the light and makes seeing possible—the scenes that the periaktoi
present—is also that which is itself seen. The presence of the ambiguity
should prompt us to ask not how to insert vision into blind eyes, or

even draw out the vision that the soul possesses, but rather how to provide experience that re-directs everyone's vision.

Plato's suggestion for so doing can be summarized in one word: dialogue. Over and over we see the views of Socrates and others transformed as they participate in dialogue—in conversation—with one another. Indeed, we see the same thing in the classroom conversations presented earlier. But, one wonders, how do the conversations bring about the transformations—the redirecting of vision and the changing of views—that one sees taking place? I have begun to address this topic elsewhere (Haroutunian-Gordon, 1991, pp. 132–145; Haroutunian-Gordon, in press). Here, I wish to look at additional passages from the *Republic* which offer insight into the issue. The first is as follows:

> If a man were intelligent. . . he would remember that there are two kinds of disturbances of the eyes, stemming from two sources—when they have been transferred from light to darkness and when they have been transferred from darkness to light. And if he held that these same things happen to a soul too, whenever he saw one that is confused and unable to make anything out, he wouldn't laugh without reasoning but would go on to consider whether, come from a brighter life, it is in darkness for want of being accustomed, or whether, going from greater lack of learning to greater brightness, it is dazzled by the greater brilliance. And then he would deem the first soul happy for its condition and its life, while he would pity the second. . . . And if he wanted to laugh at the second soul, his laughing in this case would be less a laugh of scorn than would his laughing at the soul that has come from above out of the light. (518a–b)

When Socrates says that confusion arises from two sources—moving from a brighter place to a darker one and vice versa—he seems to mean that understanding is a matter of adjustment to conditions. To be "dazzled" or "unaccustomed to darkness" is to be so poorly adjusted to the circumstances that seeing is impossible. The remedy for either condition, then, is to become adjusted—to shift one's way of seeing so that conditions are not blinding and vision can be drawn out.

The two sources of confusion—moving from darkness to light and vice versa—are not equally objectionable, however. In the latter instance the soul, while confused is, nevertheless, "happy," while in the former case, the soul is to be pitied. Furthermore, while the former might deserve a laugh of scorn, the latter would not. Why does Socrates make such claims? The answer is perhaps suggested in the following passage,

again from the *Republic,* where he addresses the guardians in the context
of comments to Glaucon about the ideal city:

> But you [that] we have begotten for yourselves and for the rest
> of the city like leaders and kings in hives. So you must go down,
> each in his turn, into the common dwelling of the others and
> get habituated along with them to seeing the dark things. And,
> in getting habituated to it, you will see ten thousand times
> better than the men there, and you'll know what each of the
> phantoms is, and of what it is a phantom, because you have
> seen the truth about fair, just, and good things. (520 b–c)

The soul that has seen the light and must thus adjust to darkness is
preferable to one which is dazzled, for the former has a perspective
with which to view the "phantoms" or appearances. Its "adjustment"
to the conditions of darkness, then, involves putting that which it sees
into perspective so that "[it] knows what each of the phantoms is and
of what it is a phantom." The soul, which can take such perspective
and can differentiate between that which seems to be and that which
is "happy" precisely because it cannot be misled by that which only
seems to be "fair, just, and good." Such a soul, if confused for a while
by darkness to which it is unaccustomed, might be worthy of scorn
if its actions be inappropriate to the situation in which it finds itself.
Plato taught that all wrongdoing was involuntary and that virtue is
insight, knowledge. No one, Plato felt, would do evil knowingly, so
bad people acted only out of the ignorance of an unilluminated soul,
that is, one that lacks vision of "the Good."[3]

In the allegory of the cave Plato likens the illumination of "the good"
to that of the sun. But the soul that has never seen the light deserves
pity rather than scorn, for it has little hope of adjusting its vision so
as to distinguish appearance from reality. As it has never seen the light,
it must remain in a permanent state of bedazzlement, as it lacks
perspective from which to judge appearances.

Upon reading these lines from Plato, one is perhaps inclined to
draw analogies between students and those in a state of bedazzlement—those in the cave who have never been exposed to the light—
and between teachers and those who have been allowed to leave the
cave and contemplate the "brightest regions of being." The students,
then would seem to be in need of *instruere*—in need of being furnished
with the knowledge and skills that the teachers possess, having been
exposed to the truth. Indeed, as noted at the outset, the modern vision
of education locates the source of truth in the teacher, so that the failure
of education today is said to be the failure to impart to students that

which teachers know and students do not know. The foregoing analysis, however, suggests that such a view is inadequate.

To see why with yet greater precision, let us note one more point that Socrates makes to Glaucon in the *Republic*:

> [Glaucon] Do you mean to say that we must do them [those who have ventured out of the cave into the light] this wrong, and compel them to live an inferior life when the better is in their power?
> [Socrates] You have again forgotten, my friend, said I, that the law is not concerned with the special happiness of any class in the state, but is trying to produce this condition in the city as a whole, harmonizing and adapting the citizens to one another by persuasion and compulsion, and requiring them to impart to one another any benefit which they are severally able to bestow upon the community, and that it itself creates such men in the state, not that it may allow each to take what course pleases him, but with a view to using them for the binding together of the commonwealth. (519e–520a)

Here, Socrates tells Glaucon that those who have "seen the light," are obliged to return to the darkness of the cave to "take charge of the other citizens and to be their guardians" (520a). The obligation exists because the "binding together of the commonwealth" requires it. The city, says Socrates, cannot thrive if the "special happiness" available to some is not made available to all.

But the passage says more as well. The spreading of the "special happiness" throughout the city (i.e., the larger community) comes from "harmonizing and adapting the citizens to one another by persuasion and compulsion." Now, given the context, it seems reasonable to assume that the "harmonizing and adapting" affects all the citizens—both those who have been out of the cave and those who have not. Furthermore, the "harmonizing and adapting" would seem to take place through the dialogue that occurs between the cave dwellers and those who have returned from the outside—between the students and the teachers, if you will.

How will the dialogue harmonize and adapt the participants? Those who return to the cave, having ventured outside, speak to the cave dwellers about the meaning of the "phantoms" or images that appear on the walls of the cave. The cave dwellers must be "persuaded and compelled" by the stories that they hear. They answer—agree or disagree, or perhaps they raise questions and offer alternative stories themselves. Their ideas about the meaning are "drawn out" as the conversation proceeds. Likewise, the meaning of the images for those who view them from the perspective that the "truth" affords also shifts: it becomes "harmonized" and "adapted" as the views of other discussants are heard, for these help one to see the worth of one's interpretations and perhaps additional aspects of the perspective or "truth" that is brought to the situation. As the ideas of all the participants in the conversation change, they become "harmonized and adapted" to one another: they come to hold more beliefs in common, and so can act in greater consort with one another. If *educare* has been effective, the beliefs which have been drawn out of the participants will enable them to live more happily than was previously possible.

Having briefly explored Socrates' view of how dialogue between people transforms the vision of all participants, let us conclude by underscoring one of the points he makes. The power of the conversation described in the preceding paragraph derives from several sources, one of which is the fact that some of the participants have been allowed to leave the dark regions of the cave, and to adjust their vision so as to tolerate the light and contemplate the "brightest regions of being," where the "truth" may be discerned. Now, if these same participants are said to be teachers, then it behooves us to make available opportunities to venture forth out of the cave and into "the city," the community of educators. Rud and Oldendorf (1992) put this suggestion in modern guise in describing the work of The North Carolina Center for the Advancement of Teaching:

> We believe that our elementary and secondary teachers should be given the opportunity to take charge of their own growth and development...to pursue their own intellectual and creative interests, free from the structure of tests, grades, or follow-up classroom checks. We are firm in the belief that meaningful staff development begins with intellectual, artistic, and moral growth. (p. xi)

One might argue that as teachers pursue the interests that stir their passions, they are drawn out of the cave: The scene before them shifts so that the meaning of their activities changes and the understanding of their value and significance deepens. This is a very different image of the teacher as professional envisioned when we seek to *instruct* prospective teachers in the rules and principles of the "knowledge base" of teaching determined by educational researchers. As we ponder the reforms needed in teacher preparation, we might consider offering both novice and experienced educators many more opportunities to draw out and develop their personal interests—even those which seem unrelated to their teaching.[4] For in so doing, we may provide them with chances to examine that which appears to be true in the new light to which one becomes adjusted over a long period of exposure. Under such conditions, readjustment of personal and professional vision can take place, together with a turning of the soul, so that the truth about appearances may be seen. Who among us would not wish to be taught by such a soul?

CHAPTER 8

Some Thoughts on Privacy in Classrooms

_____ C. J. B. Macmillan

Classrooms are public places. Indeed, an institution that did not bring groups of students together for pedagogical interchanges and dialogue wouldn't be recognizable as a school; it is of the institution's nature that learning—not to say education—takes place in groups. The social decision to use schools in the education of children is significant not only for financial reasons; a public dimension is added to education when children are engaged in classroom life.

For John Dewey this was centrally important; education, he argued, is inherently social, in both aims and means. For him, schools serve social or community purposes and should stand as an idealized version of the community as a whole.[1] Dewey's vision is part of his view of democracy: "A democracy is more than a form of government; it is primarily a mode of associated living, of conjoint communicated experience" (1916, p. 87). Although we might imagine Dewey arguing for the provision of privacy for students, his emphasis upon the shared quality of democracy—and of education—leaves little room for such a concern.

Nonetheless, there are reasons to be concerned about privacy in classrooms. E. Z. Friedenberg put it well in 1965:

> After the family, the school is the first social institution an individual must deal with—the place in which he learns to handle himself with strangers. The school establishes the pattern of his subsequent assumptions as to which relations between the individual and society are appropriate and which constitute invasions of privacy and constraints on his spirit— what the British, with exquisite precision, call "taking a liberty." (p. 44)

In further comments, Friedenberg insults the public school's "contempt for personal privacy and individual autonomy" (p. 44) and its "diffuse willingness to mind everybody's business but its own" (p. 47).

I will argue that privacy has a central place in all educational contexts, but that that place is not the same as more ordinary pedagogical procedures. A criticism of a school for not respecting students' privacy is quite different from one that attacks it for not achieving pedagogical goals like instruction in knowledge of history, spelling, or the ability to write well.

First we must ask why a school's or teacher's lack of concern for the privacy of its students should be viewed as a fault rather than a strength. Isn't the crucial concern to develop students who put the good of the society or culture—the "public" perhaps—above their private well being? Shouldn't a public institution and its agents be concerned with the public good rather than the private benefits individual students might gain there? Privacy, it might be argued, is anathema in such an institution. In schools at any rate, there should be no "right" to privacy.

This argument pits the individual against society and assumes that a concern for the social good cannot develop if the individual is treated as the (logically) primary element in a social/individual dualism or dichotomy. Rampant individualism with no moral content, no connection with the social system as a whole, leaves lonely people with no moral basis for support of their own selves and no way of making meaningful connections with other people. They are merely bound morally by external laws and customs.

Bellah and his colleagues (Bellah et al., 1985) have considered the place of the individual in modern American society. In their analysis, we have inadequate moral vocabularies (and hence, social practices) to provide an ethical footing for the development of a viable picture either of the individual or of a morally significant society, to say nothing of the relations between individual and society. The remedy for this lack is, in their view, a "revitalized social ecology" (pp. 283–290) that includes new ways of thinking of individualism and the social system. This would not be easy, as they say, since

> such a change involves a deep cultural, social, and even psychological transformation that is not to be brought about by expert fine-tuning of economic institutions alone. On the contrary, at every point, institutional changes, educational changes, and motivational changes would go hand in hand. (p. 289)

How does privacy fit into such a picture? On the one hand, it could be held that promoting privacy in schools—and elsewhere—would support the current unhealthy emphasis upon the lonely individual who lives only for personal pleasures (where dope is as "valuable" as self-knowledge), whose private life is totally divorced from his or her public life at work and in the politics of the country. Insofar as there is any right to privacy, it would seem to be empty of content or of moral significance.

On the other hand, it might be argued that despite the public nature of schools and classrooms, the youngest kindergartner does not leave the right to privacy at the classroom door. Insofar as privacy can be considered a right of individuals, it should apply to children as well as to adults—perhaps even more so, since it is in childhood that we become aware of and used to the conditions under which we will live as adults. Few rights are inalienable, however, and there are circumstances in which even the right to privacy might be trumped by overarching rights and purposes. The question here is the extent to which the child's right to privacy can justifiably be abrogated in classrooms.

Freidenberg's comments assume that his enemy believes that the individual's privacy is to be sacrificed to the public good, to the school's ideas and ideals of what good citizenship amounts to. The general theme of his work suggests that any abrogation of privacy by teachers or school routines is to be avoided if children's talents are not to be squashed by the schools. The implicit elitism of Friedenberg's views may work against acceptance of his own criticism. It isn't because of any recognized rights of all individuals that he seems to be concerned with privacy in schools. Rather, his almost Nietzschean view justifies privacy by the development of the specially talented and sensitive.

If we are to see the point of teachers' respecting privacy in schools, we need a "theory" that brings the pedagogical or educational concerns of the institution into line with a respect for students' privacy.

Jeffrey Reiman (1976) suggests what might be called an "educational" reason for respecting privacy in classrooms. To show what his thesis is, it is necessary to consider his analysis of privacy:

> Privacy is a social practice. It involves a complex of behaviors that stretches from refraining from asking questions about what is none of one's business to refraining from looking into open windows one passes on the street, from refraining from entering a closed door without knocking to refraining from knocking down a locked door without a warrant. (p. 310)

It is important to emphasize that privacy is not viewed as the individual's merely being alone, or even being left alone. It is part of a host of ways of acting hospitably toward others and of expectations about others' actions toward oneself. It is embedded in related *social* practices and may well be expressed as a right when considered as a legal or moral matter.

The central importance of privacy, though, is spelled out at more length by Reiman:

> Privacy can in this sense be looked at as a very complicated social ritual. But what is its point? In response I want to defend the following thesis. *Privacy is a social ritual by means of which an individual's moral title to his existence is conferred.* Privacy is an essential part of the complex social practice by means of which the social group recognizes—and communicates to the individual—that his existence is his own. And this is a precondition of personhood. (Reiman, 1976, p. 310. Emphasis in the original.)

This rather mysterious notion—that an individual's "moral title to his existence" is conferred by the social practice of privacy—depends upon a particular version of personhood:

> To be a person, an individual must recognize not just his actual capacity to shape his destiny by his choices. He must also recognize that he has an exclusive moral right to shape his destiny. And this in turn presupposes that he believes that the concrete reality which he is, and through which his destiny is realized, belongs to him in a moral sense. (Reiman, 1976, p. 310)

This is an adult picture, however; that person is not a child, dependent upon adults for her current destiny, perhaps not able to foresee that there is a destiny to be shaped. Here, privacy can be seen as a practice or "social ritual" that "confirms, and demonstrates respect for, the personhood of already developed persons" (p. 310). But there is another side to it.

> *And* if one takes—as I am inclined to—the symbolic interactionist perspective which teaches that "selves" are created in social interaction rather than flowering innately from inborn seeds, to this claim is added an even stronger one: privacy is necessary to the creation of *selves* out of human beings, since a self is at least in part a human being who regards his existence—his thoughts, his body, his actions—as his *own*. (Reiman, 1976, p. 310. Emphasis in the original.)

The full educational—or pedagogical—force of this notion can now be spelled out: without the social practice of privacy, children do not get their society's or community's recognition of them as morally significant. They do not develop *as persons*. "The social ritual of privacy seems to be an essential ingredient in the process by which 'persons' are created out of prepersonal infants" (Reiman, 1976, p. 310). In sum, "privacy is a condition of the original and continuing creation of 'selves' or 'persons' " (p. 310). Similarly, without the social practice of privacy *in the school*, teachers cannot develop as *professional* persons.

Reiman's is a remarkably potent vision of the importance of privacy in the moral lives of individuals. It goes against what might be considered a "weak" or "etiquette" version of privacy. In this weak version, we are tempted to view respect for other persons' privacy merely as a matter of etiquette, of manners. We don't interfere in others' lives because, like picking up the outside fork first, that's the way it's done here.

A person who has no respect for rules of etiquette is no fun to be around; we might shun him. But the quality of shunning is different from that appropriate to the person who (e.g.) cares little for the hurt he does to others. We don't condemn rudeness as moral transgression. Neither do we view *particular* rules of etiquette as central to the personhood of individuals. The weak version would have us criticize one who does not respect the privacy of another as if he had not held the door of the car for a lady. But it is much more important than this.

Reiman shows us how simpering such a weak version is, how widely it misses the moral and educational mark. And it shows us a way to connect the social (and educational) practice of privacy with the concerns of *Habits of the Heart* (1985). While it sounds as if the social practice of privacy might lead only to a reinforcement of the empty individualism that Bellah and his colleagues find so prevalent in American society, Reiman ties privacy up closely with the development of the moral personhood that is central to their position.

If privacy provides no specific content except the individual's sense of self, no commitment to broader social purposes or contexts, it could not give any sort of basis for the new social ecology Bellah and his colleagues argue is necessary. But the individualists of the Bellah picture have no strong sense of self; they belong to the "me generation" without ways of seeing themselves as moral beings in a moral context.

> If there are vast numbers of a selfish, narcissistic "me generation" in America, we did not find them, but we certainly did find that the language of individualism, the primary American language of self-understanding, limits the ways in which people think. (Bellah et al., 1985, p. 290)

In part, the Reiman view provides the moral basis for a language of individualism that goes beyond the emptiness of the psycho-babble that passes for self-understanding, for it is embedded in social practices that support the moral nature of the individual-in-society.

It also sets up a *prima facie* right to privacy in schools for both teachers and students, at least in those who see their mission as involving the development of morally autonomous persons. A school that serves only a training function might bypass such a right; or one that views its task as brainwashing or extreme indoctrination might intentionally ignore the practice of privacy in order to achieve its (immoral) ends. But I trust that this is not the school with which we are concerned.

The task that now faces us is to see what the classroom and schoolhouse payoff of this position amounts to. What practices are implied by such a view? Are there any pedagogical goals or other "habits of the heart" that would give reason for ignoring or abrogating students' rights to privacy?

It is tempting, for example, to think of privacy merely as a physical thing—being alone—and to suggest that there be little holes or boxes in which children could hide from their classmates. On the other hand, it might be that one would think of privacy solely in terms of keeping information about students out of the hands of unauthorized others. Both of these are possibilities, of course, but they only begin to scratch the surface.

In one of the best discussions of privacy in classroom contexts, Joanne Reynolds (1966) never quite argues that privacy is connected with personhood. She does say this: "If, then, as shall be assumed in this paper, we accept children as persons in their own right, rather than as slaves or as property then they are entitled to the same courtesies and respect which are afforded to adults" (p. 257). This is an argument that children are to be treated as persons and that this involves respecting their rights to privacy *if* they have them. She considers legal, psychological, religious, and moral grounds for children's rights (pp. 256–257), but her argument is cast in the subjunctive mode—she never provides the arguments for accepting those grounds. Reynolds does discuss five areas in which privacy in classrooms should be considered: Protection of [children's] private property; providing individual solitude for children; freedom from surreptitious observation; exercise of choice regarding disclosure of personal thoughts, feelings, and data; and individual children's control over the tangible products of their thought and imagination. I don't want to repeat her discussion, which is as pertinent today as it was thirty years ago. But some special areas might be taken up as examples.

Privacy becomes a problem when otherwise legitimate pedagogical goals and procedures seem to require making things public that might otherwise remain private. My interest in this topic, for example, was reawakened when a student in a graduate class in philosophy of education recalled her elementary school years with horror: she had been required to take part in spelling bees, an experience that left her "humiliated and upset."[2] In recalling this, she condemned the teacher for not respecting her privacy. It wasn't that she was a bad speller exposing her ignorance for all to see; indeed, she claimed to have been a rather good speller—but in the context of a spelling bee, she lost her abilities, spelled wrong, and was seated almost immediately. "What," she asked, "was learned by this exposure?" The relationship between teacher and student should be private, she claimed. Her objection to spelling bees finally amounted to a cry against an attack on her very being.

There was an irony in this, for this was a music education student. Try to imagine a teaching field that requires *less* public performance in order for proper teaching to take place. Yet the horror remains for anyone sensitive to such matters. In some sense, a teacher who requires a student unwillingly to exhibit her knowledge (or lack of it) publicly does something that seems *prima facie* wrong. We are at the least tempted to say that that teacher has breached the student's right to privacy. We can arrive at a more sympathetic understanding of the student's position, including the student teacher, by considering the social relation between teacher and school administration. Consider the horror of a principal walking into a class unexpectedly.

But surely if there must be public criteria for such things as people's pains (Wittgenstein, 1953), there must equally be public criteria for educational achievements. There can (logically) be no teaching if there is no way in which the teacher can assess how well the students are doing with the subject that is the focus of their interaction, or any good teaching that cannot be assessed, at least in part, by an administrator.[3] This suggests that whenever teachers and students interact pedagogically, there must be some "public" exemplification of the students' achievement. So a teacher cannot be *blamed* for having students demonstrate their achievements: it is a necessity. But there's public and "public" here. Tests of spelling ability, which might be written spelling tests, examination of other written work, or even a clever multiple choice examination, can be seen as public criteria in the sense that the results are shared with the teacher who uses them in further teaching of that student. The teacher and student together might know the score without letting others know. They are alone together, as it were. The spelling bee is only one way of getting at such matters, usually instituted for reasons other than testing. The problem with many teacher evaluation systems is that a *formative* assessment, meant to improve practice, is used *summatively* to determine issues such as salaries and promotion.

But there are limits even to teacher-student "private" sharing. It is becoming common for teachers of writing (and many other subjects) to require their students to keep journals that are then read by the teacher as part of the assessment procedure. The goal in journal-keeping is worthy: students who get in the habit of writing about their experience not only gain fluency in writing but also come to understand themselves and their subject-matter better. Imagine, though, the student who, believing that the journal is private, reports all her innermost thoughts and outermost actions in her journal; those actions and thoughts might disturb the teacher—perhaps they include confessions of child-abuse or drug use. Caught on the horns of a professional dilemma, the teacher might feel it necessary to make that information public, or even merely to talk professionally with the student about the contents of her journal. No longer are the teacher and student alone together, for there are other responsibilities that the teacher—as both teacher and public functionary—cannot overlook.

This suggests that there must be limits to the use of journals in such contexts; in part this is because in order to respect the students' privacy teachers might find themselves in an ethical bind. Either they live within the bounds of the social practice of privacy in their work or they find themselves ignoring other responsibilities to their students and the society at large. Put this way, it looks as if respecting privacy is merely a more or less technical matter, though. For there are ways in which teachers might give the journal assignment that announce that the materials will not be private, or that the journal should be limited to matters that the students would not mind making public. Teachers could balance the interests of privacy against pedagogical necessity.

Both of these instances suggest a dimension of privacy in pedagogical reasoning that might be missed. Privacy is both a means and an end in classroom practices. By this I mean that the social practice of privacy can be viewed as a means to the development of self stressed by Reiman. It can also be seen as a goal to be achieved in classroom practices that aim at other complex goals. A spelling bee, perhaps, aims at (a) improving students' spelling abilities as well as (b) students' abilities to perform in front of others, (c) the development of a spirit of interpersonal competition, and (d) the development of team spirit in the classroom. The first of these might be called a "subject-matter" goal, the last three "character" goals, since they aim at qualities of the character of the classroom and of individual students.

On the face of it, privacy could conflict only with the last three of this complex of goals. This is because privacy, like these three, is a social practice with a justifying result rather than an end to be achieved by pedagogical methods. We justify such methods by the learning that they help teachers and students achieve; pedagogically, a spelling bee is justified by how well it helps students learn to spell, and an in-class teacher performance measure by how well it *helps* teachers learn to teach. As a punishment and reward system, it may be misplaced. But pedagogical methods are (morally) criticized by how well—or badly— they help in achieving the other things that we expect of classroom teaching—such things as competitiveness, honesty, courage, kindness, and a host of other personal virtues.[4]

Question: Could there ever be a conflict between privacy and pedagogical goals? Interestingly, this is like asking whether there could be a conflict between treating students honestly and teaching them history. They are different categories of concern in classrooms. One could try to justify treating students honestly by appealing to some characteristic of the students that would be achieved by such treatment—but this would miss the moral point of honesty itself as a moral practice. Or consider the moral dimension of teaching and attempts to professionalize teachers via a "knowledge base." Similarly with privacy. To try to justify it merely as an attempt to achieve something else misses the point that it is *in* the practice (rather than *by* the practice) that the moral recognition of the students' selfhood is achieved.

If this is right, the only place in which privacy in Reiman's sense conflicts with pedagogical goals is when the teacher views her task as involved with all aspects of the students' character, i.e., when the teacher believes that it is the teacher's task to be such a part of her students' lives that nothing is to be sacred to the individual. Such a teacher stops at nothing, sees no limits to the professional responsibilities. And in a very important sense, that teacher, who may care very much for the students, has no respect for them as moral beings. Nor do administrators who try to manage every detail of their teachers' lives and practice.

It is possible or even probable that privacy might conflict with the practice of other moral habits or virtues like honesty, kindness, and even competitiveness. Teachers who stress the development of a competitive spirit in their students might, for example, ignore the complaints of my student that individual privacy was not being respected. And we might criticize such teachers for not having weighed the development of students' sense of self against the development of a particular type of character in the students. Think of what happens to cooperation among teachers when competitive evaluation leads to public rewards.

It is beyond the scope of this chapter to consider all of the facets of the development of virtue. Pincoffs (1986) provides an excellent introduction to the topic, with a possible weighting of different virtues that teachers should consider as they decide on pedagogical methods. What should not be forgotten is that the social practice of privacy—even in classrooms—may be a moral floor beneath any consideration of other moral qualities. Without that sense of oneself as a moral being, it is hard to see how openmindedness, responsibility, honesty, hospitality, and other virtues can be achieved.

CHAPTER 9

Learning in Comfort: Developing an Ethos of Hospitality in Education

_____ *Anthony G. Rud Jr.*

The word "hospitality" conjures up several associations. We may think of the literary conventions of hospitality so important in medieval French romances, our present-day "hospitality industry," or as Henri Nouwen says, "(a) soft sweet kindness, tea parties, bland conversations and a general atmosphere of coziness" (1975, p. 66). I argue for something quite different. Learning in comfort and trust is a neglected facet of our schools and a "gap" in our understanding and appreciation of the conditions of teaching and learning.

The combination of learning and hospitality comes from several sources. I begin by exploring its connection in the life of the Benedictine monastery, where I shall report on a study visit I made to gauge the value of hospitality toward oneself, and to experience the coupling of learning and hospitality. I focus on how being a host in a learning environment is a theme in several contemporary writers by beginning with an analysis of Henri Nouwen's (1975) claims for hospitality and teaching. Turning next to the work of Parker Palmer (1983), I investigate the ethical and epistemological aspects of hospitality in an educational setting. I consider Henry David Thoreau's insights into hospitality that appear in *Walden* (1854; 1983), and throughout I discuss parallels in educational practice. In the final section, I move to a broader consideration of a particular kind of education in a vision of a good society. Michael Ignatieff's treatment of the "needs of strangers" (1984) and Dewey's conception of democracy as a way of living (1916; 1980) shed light upon a wider framework for seeking why this gap occurs, and for proposing means for its closure.

I

A former colleague had mentioned to me the Benedictine tradition of hospitality and learning, and how it was related to our work in professional development and renewal of career teachers. This piqued my interest in learning firsthand more about the monastic life. I wanted to find out whether monastic practices could be secularized and applied to the schools, and how such practices could serve as metaphoric bridges to my own thinking. I visited a session in a program for teachers on the idea of the "cell" in all its scientific and metaphoric variations. One morning, two monks from nearby Belmont Abbey described their way of life in the monastic "cell." I wanted to see this life with my own eyes, so I arranged for a visit.

Heading up Interstate 85 toward Charlotte, North Carolina, I steel myself for what I anticipate lies before me. This had been a particularly difficult autumn. October is always frantic with activities for educators. Having one of our cars towed to the garage twice in two days heightens my desire to find a cool shaded spot for the soul. I fill the state car with shock waves of regressive, power-pop anthems—Heart's Wilson sisters wail from the rear speakers as I speed toward the abbey. The abbey sits just a few hundred yards from I-85, which swells and roars with the commerce of Charlotte, our junior Atlanta lying just 10 miles east.

Abbot Oscar Burnett greets me. A short man with thick glasses, he is warm and friendly as he helps me find my room in the cloister. The abbey is tastefully designed and very 1990s—exposed brick, hardwood floors, track lighting, and potted plants. The black metal window frames and smoked glass remind me of Brightleaf Square, a converted tobacco warehouse filled with shops for gourmet coffee and Italian toothpaste, in Durham, North Carolina. My room is long and narrow; despite the din from the interstate, it is remarkably calm. Burnett tells me of his thirty-five years at the monastery and how he had been a lawyer in Savannah before entering the order. I marvel at the Benedictine vow of stability to remain in one place and devote themselves to a life of prayer and service.

I ask the abbot some preliminary questions about hospitality and learning. He is keen to tell me that hospitality is not like a "happy hour." Burnett feels it is important not to be sentimental, despite the Benedictine pledge to receive the guest as Christ. One must learn to help those who come to join the order, as well as guests like me, to distinguish between wants and needs, for these are usually different.

Later, in talking to Brother Arthur Pendleton during lunch, I learn that the rules for treating guests have been modified and interpreted. Abbots no longer wash the feet of guests (Fry, 1982, p. 74), but the emphasis remains on listening first. As the conversation changes, Brother Arthur, a professor of chemistry at adjoining Belmont Abbey College, launches into an unexpected discussion of the upcoming

National Council for Accreditation of Teacher Education (NCATE) site visit. He is among the faculty leaders trying to wed Benedictine precepts, particularly the commandment to listen first, with teacher education.

At lunch, I meet Paul Krebs, another guest. Like me, he is a late thirty-something father with a demanding job. He is here on the urging of his wife for a four-day visit. Paul says that he is very goal and task oriented, always making lists of things to do. Sometimes he stops and wonders what he has really accomplished; he thinks that love, of family and of God, is what is really important. As we sit under the magnolia trees on a clear, cool fall day, I recognize myself in him, and in what he says. Though I do not share Paul's deep religious conviction, I see how he aims to be hospitable to himself first in preparation to receive others.

That afternoon, I take a long walk and spend the rest of the day lying in bed, coming to terms with my surroundings. I fight off the urge to read materials I had brought from work. I want to try to see and experience my surroundings with fresh, unburdened eyes. I feel myself chafing under the routine as we chant psalms. I take meals and go to church with the monks. A famous scene in Victor Hugo's *Les Misérables* (1862; 1979), when Jean Valjean can find no quarter for his first night of freedom, enters my thoughts. The bishop receives Valjean with uncommon grace; the bishop has his table set with silver for six, though only the two will dine. The depth of the bishop's hospitality toward a stranger is emphasized when the bishop later accepts that Jean Valjean stole the silver during the night.

I begin to see how the strict routine and emphasis upon prayer and study could prepare one for a life of service and of hospitality toward oneself and to another. The Benedictine vow of stability permits the acceptance of boundaries within which the individual can grow. I recognize, too, the major emphasis upon listening among the Benedictines. With the help of Brother Arthur, I see how listening indeed has importance for how one teaches, and for teacher education. When you listen to a student, the student becomes the teacher. This reversal of roles is important for teachers to realize, to allow their own learning, and to put oneself in the role of the student.

Yet in a sense both tragic and ironic as given by other authors in this volume, I never did fully achieve the listening to oneself so important to my conception of hospitality in learning. I struggled toward my goal. I came to realize my limitations within the monastic confines, and that tempers my views toward teaching and learning. My venture was ironic, because, as many others before me have noted, to know oneself should be the easiest of tasks (after all, who would know you better?), but this goal can also prove to be insurmountable. The goal of listening to oneself, crucial as it is to teaching and learning, is a tragic goal in that it can never be fully achieved, and is an ironic goal in that it has to be attempted at all.

II

Listening, first to oneself, can allow one to listen to others, whether the "other" is a human being or another part of the natural world. Henry David Thoreau's withdrawal to the woods of Walden Pond allowed him to learn, in solitude, to be at home with himself.[1] Thoreau takes an interest in his own life, and enjoins us to take an interest in our own lives as well (Cavell, 1974). Thoreau had his share of visitors during his sojourn; many were the restless and frazzled men whom Alexis de Tocqueville saw as typically American in his earlier sojourn in our country. These men could never be alone in the woods by Walden Pond (Thoreau, 1854; 1983, p. 198). Thoreau sought to alert us to pay attention to the strangeness in our own lives, and to recover from that strangeness as from a disease (Cavell, 1974, pp. 54, 79).

Such listening is an important part of the pedagogy developed by Max van Manen (1991). He stresses that the German and Dutch term "pedagogy" is more broadly construed than our more restrictive term "curriculum and instruction." Deeper than an instrumental view of teaching as merely imparting information or developing skills, the idea of pedagogy developed by van Manen has a strong connection to parenting, and being present for the pupil in mind, soul, and body. Such teaching is a vocation or calling, thoroughly infused with prior and necessary normative concerns. One cannot be a teacher without a "mindfulness" toward children (van Manen, 1991, p. 9), something all the techniques of teaching and classroom management cannot give. Pedagogical understanding is the active branch of thoughtfulness, which itself is a reflection upon a teaching and learning situation. What van Manen calls pedagogical "tact" is the realization of pedagogical understanding in practice. Van Manen's tact, with its bodily signs of eye contact and modulated voice, forms the manner of hospitality in teaching and learning.

III

Hospitality. . . means primarily the creation of a free space where the stranger can enter and become a friend instead of an enemy. Hospitality is not to change people, but to offer them space where change can take place. . .Teaching, therefore, asks first of all the creation of a space where students and teachers can enter into a fearless communication with each other and allow their respective life experiences to be their primary and most valuable source of growth and maturation. . .The hospitable teacher has to reveal to students that they have something to offer. . .A good host is the one who believes that his guest is carrying a promise he wants to reveal to anyone who shows a genuine interest. (Nouwen, 1975, pp. 71, 85, 87)

As for Thoreau, one's own strangeness, and the strangers one meets in life, are themes for Henri Nouwen's discussion of hospitality. Hospitality for Nouwen comes under the second of three movements of the spiritual life, "From Hostility to Hospitality," (chapter 4). What precedes the move toward hospitality to others is similar to what both Thoreau and the Benedictines stress: the achievement of a hospitality toward and knowledge of oneself. Hospitable acts create an emptiness that would then allow the world and strangers to speak to oneself, and one can listen and hear them (p. 72). Noddings, in discussing Simone Weil, speaks of how "the soul empties itself of all its own contents in order to receive the other" (1992, p. 16). Strangers, most importantly including oneself, can "cast off their strangeness and become our fellow human beings" (Nouwen, 1975, p. 65), in a climate for hospitality characterized by solitude and poverty (pp. 102–103), in other words, simplicity of manner and mode of living. This is most difficult in a world where even in a monastic cell I was tempted to fill time and attention with lists of things to do.

Much as Max van Manen sees "tact" as a unifying idea for his pedagogy, Nouwen uses hospitality to unite different modes of interpersonal relationships. He treats three "forms of hospitality," between parents and children, teachers and students, and professionals and patients. I shall concentrate my attention on the teacher-student relationship, and how hospitality works there.

Many students learn quickly that school is a place of routine and obligation rather than openness and wonder. School is often a show-place of what Foucault (1979) calls "disciplinary technology." Growth in learning and spirit is frequently sacrificed for an accumulation of grades, credits, and other badges of merit. With some bright exceptions, many schools mirror our production-oriented society. Nouwen talks about the role of the teacher in such a world. There is little encouragement for Benedictine listening here; rather authoritative professional expertise and discipline are in order.

The power relations within schools between administrators and teachers are facets of this disciplinary technology. Teachers must be "accountable" for student learning, and if their students slip, heads often roll. I know of a superintendent who proudly keeps a "war room," much like General Schwarzkopf's bunker in Riyadh, where test scores of his schools are charted on the wall. Should a principal fall behind, he or she is summoned to the superintendent's summer boot camp for retraining. Yet the wisest teachers know that even in spite of such punitive accountability, they will learn much from their students. If one casts off the mantle of pedagogical invincibility, a teacher probably learns more from students than students learn from the teacher.

Nouwen (1975) reminds us that ". . .students are not just the poor, needy, ignorant beggars who come to the man or woman of knowledge, but that they are indeed like guests who honor the house with their visit and will not leave it without having made their own contribution" (p. 89). Guests are always temporary passers-by in our lives, or at least we often hope so. As such, they cannot be fully molded, and so the same for students (p. 92). Similarly, Nicholas Burbules reminds us earlier in this volume of what he calls the "tragic" nature of the teaching situation, where teachers acknowledge and accept such limitations in what they can do for students.

IV

The downfall of many tragic heroes was *hubris,* or arrogant pride. These literary heroes did not realize their limitations. Many of us have now developed such arrogance to a complete epistemology and way of being in the world. At the heart of Parker Palmer's book (1983) is an argument to overcome this mode of knowing, which he calls "objectivism" (p. 27), whereby humans believe that the world is a group of discrete objects "out there" to be manipulated toward human ends. Palmer argues for a "wholesight" (p. xii) of heart and mind, and for pedagogies that would accomplish it. Palmer justifies wholesight as it is the *only* way we can come fully to know ourselves. It is a recovery of knowing as an act of love and connection with others and with the natural world (p. 9).

Palmer treats hospitality as both an ethical and epistemological idea. Let us first clarify his epistemology a bit more. For Palmer, truth is not out there, and importantly, it is not solely within ourselves either. He goes between the poles of objectivism and subjectivism by locating truth and knowledge in relationships, where the outside world meets and mediates our own workings (p. 54). Like Martin Buber's (1970) I-thou ontology, relation is characterized by immediacy and presence. We seek to know the world and others, and thus come to know ourselves.

The Benedictine monks at Belmont Abbey open their lives in a quest for knowledge. The late author Norman Maclean strives for the same in his recent book, *Young Men and Fire* (1992). The story of the tragic fire in Montana's Mann Gulch is as much something out there as it is the telling of Maclean's search for his own knowledge of life's terrors and mysteries. Maclean's many years spent ruminating over the event in Mann Gulch underscores just how difficult the attainment of such knowledge is.

Palmer's (1983) pedagogy derives from this view of knowledge. Teaching must be a creation of a space where enactment of personal knowledge and an opening to other beings is possible (p. 69). *Openness*, *boundaries*, and *hospitality* characterize this learning space (p. 71). Like Nouwen, Palmer believes that a receptivity toward strange ideas and their bearers is central to such teaching. But an indiscriminate openness, without what Nouwen calls "confrontation" (1975, p. 98), may be just as bad as manipulative objectivism or murky subjectivism. One can only be receptive to what is done within limits or boundaries, and one must be a presence to let others know who we are ("An empty house is not a hospitable house" [Nouwen, 1975, p. 99]). The firm boundaries of the monastic life hold the monks within so that, as Palmer (1983) says, "truth can do its work" (p. 73), where learning is not painless, but rather the painful is made possible (p. 74).

Palmer's epistemology is relevant to how the legacy of Socrates fits into our treatment of hospitality and education. On the surface, at least, it seems that the well-known interrogative style of Socrates is inhospitable. Closer inspection shows that this is the case only if we fall back into hackneyed, shallow conceptions of hospitality, as "happy hour" filled with "soft sweet kindness." Socrates engaged others in such confrontation, taking seriously their ideas and trying to find, with them, truth. In proclaiming his own ignorance, and entreating others to follow him in seeking the truth, Socrates helped create the space where at once one knew who he was (despite his claim of ignorance) and where the pain of learning was made possible, at least for some of the people Socrates encountered.

V

Palmer (1983) advocates becoming full partners with one's students (pp. 103–104). In order to face one's ignorance with humility and see that we are all students as well as teachers, he suggests teaching often outside one's area of expertise. Yet his suggestions often go unheeded. "I went to pick up my child, and her teacher's door was locked," laments a parent I know. Hospitality, indifference, and hostility are rooted in ways that we see the world and our place in it. I want to examine briefly several programs and ideas that may be creating a more hospitable view of teaching and learning.

First, where I worked until recently, The North Carolina Center for the Advancement of Teaching (NCCAT), considers hospitality as I have described it here as a central part of its organizational theory (Rud, 1992). We provide for material comfort and collegial support within our seminar offerings for career teachers. Our pedagogy stresses Socratic discussion, experiential learning, and artistic expression. Two recent seminars on gardens invite teachers to study and appreciate, and then to create for themselves, environments in nature that allow for artistic expression. These natural creations beckon others to also come learn and create.

Just north of the main NCCAT building is a symmetrical and formal Victorian herbal garden replete with a fountain in the middle, an ironic reminder of the persistence of modernism in our postmodern age. Like the landscape design of nearby Biltmore Estate, the grounds surrounding the formal garden become wilder the further away from the building one goes. A few feet north of the garden's wooden fence, a stream comes out of the hollow. Laced with rhododendron and mountain laurel, the hollow is formed by uncultivated mountain woodland. This garden serves the same purposes as the two-hundred-year-old farmhouse in the Black Forest described by Heidegger (1977). That house was crafted to withstand natural elements, but also preserved the "childbed" and coffin within it, "and in this way it designed for the different generations under one roof the character of their journey through time" (p. 338). So, too, can the generations of teachers gather at the garden, where a token of hospitality cultivated in the ground may grant occasion for reflection upon teaching.

Second, the movement known as "invitational education" (Purkey and Novak, 1984) advocates a hospitality in learning. At the core of this view is the hypothesis that individuals have a basic need to be regarded well by others, and that we constitute ourselves in relation to others (pp. 15–16). Therefore, if we are not inviting and open to others, they cannot constitute themselves as persons, *and*, we too will be diminished. Purkey and Novak realize the importance of what they call "being personally inviting with oneself" (p. 72) as the basis of being inviting to others. One needs to treat oneself well, both physically and mentally, before one can be inviting and helpful to another. Good teaching in this view is not high test scores, but rather ". . .the process of inviting students to see themselves as able, valuable, and self-directing and of encouraging them to act in accordance with these self-perceptions" (p. xiii).

In two important works Nel Noddings (1984, 1992) develops the idea of *care* as central to both being in the world and the core of moral education (1984), and as the organizing principle behind an alternate vision of schooling (1992). Care is characterized by "engrossment or nonselective attention, and motivational displacement or the desire to help" (1992, p. 91). Care requires both openness to receive others, and an ego displacement that would allow reaching out to others.

One may ask whether students themselves have a responsibility to be hospitable. In education, at least, the onus of responsibility is upon the teacher and other educators. As Buber points out, though genuine education involves an "embracing" (umfassung) (1970, p. 178), the educative relationship is not mutual. The pupil does not embrace the teacher. In a striking passage in an essay on education (1955, p. 94) Buber claims that Eros does not have a place in education, because educators do not select their pupils, and a hallmark of an erotic relation is such selection. Thus, for Buber at least, the educative relationship is that much more difficult, for the educator must deal with the unselected students who show up on the first day of school. Here is how hospitality has primary importance.

VI

I would like to begin to sketch how this discussion of hospitality can broaden out into a view of the good society, of which schooling is an essential and integral part. Michael Ignatieff (1984) repeatedly emphasizes that the modern welfare state has taken care of our basic needs but has not recognized that satisfying these needs is not enough to provide for human flourishing. The state has mediated a "silent relationship" (p. 10) between people, so that basic needs are taken care of and we thus do not have to confront one another and meet any deeper needs than "food, shelter, clothing, warmth, and medical care" (p. 10). These deeper needs may include love, respect, honor, dignity, and solidarity with others (p. 15).

Might we not place hospitality, as described here as a *communicative* and thus also *political* virtue, as a generative quality in public life that would ground a common and democratic political involvement. By a "communicative virtue," I have in mind qualities listed recently by two theorists: "tolerance, patience, respect for differences, a willingness to listen, the inclination to admit that one may be mistaken, the ability to reinterpret or translate one's own concerns in a way that makes them comprehensible to others, the self-imposition of restraint in order that others may 'have a turn' to speak, and the disposition to express one's self honestly and sincerely" (Burbules and Rice, 1991, p. 411). These virtues give a linguistic turn to the idea of hospitality. They make dialogue possible, and thus make education possible; as Burbules and Rice claim, ". . .specifically, in education, we often need to focus more on the formation and development of particular communicative relations, devoted to inquiry and understanding, than on specific predetermined learning outcomes" (pp. 412–413). Such communicative practice is essential for democratic involvement. Let us recall Garrison's discussion of Dewey's notion of democracy being "more than a form of government; it is primarily a mode of associated living, of conjoint communicated experience" (Dewey, 1916; 1980, p. 93; cf. Noddings, 1992, pp. 10–11; and Macmillan, chapter 8). In this multiplicity of relations, where we meet in openness in the fearless communication that Nouwen describes, we can learn of others' customs, manners, and mores.

Hospitality toward self is a central aspect of the Deweyan view of teaching. It is much misunderstood, particularly by legislators and others outside the teaching profession, who believe that educational dollars and attention should focus solely on the student and the classroom. Noddings (1992) makes care for self the first of her "centers of care." Sarason (1990) examines the powerful assumption that schools "do and should exist primarily for students" (p. 136). He argues that should we not pay attention to teachers and their well-being, educational reform will fail, predictably. What I have argued is that these teachers need to pay attention to themselves to prepare to meet the challenges of making schools hospitable for students.

There are enormous hurdles to cross, in society and in our schools, before we achieve hospitality toward others. The practice of "tracking," as Jeannie Oakes reminds us, has moral as well as cognitive import (O'Neil, 1992). Young minds and hearts may be channeled into narrowness and exclusion by such practices. Noddings (1992) goes further in proposing to reorganize schools around centers of care. She addresses the moral inequities of a tracked curriculum. Yet, despite Ignatieff's warnings about slipping into utopianism, we might begin to resurrect an unsentimental language adequate to reconstitute our solidarity with others, and to express the "need for fraternity, social solidarity, [and] civic belonging" (Ignatieff, 1984, p. 138). It is in this new lexicon that hospitality, in some of its restored meanings for teaching and learning outlined here, may indeed belong.[2]

CHAPTER 10

Intellectual and Institutional Gaps in Teacher Education

Daniel P. Liston

Introduction

Jim Garrison and A.G. Rud have brought together an unusual collection of papers, a collection that highlights ideas frequently missing in our educational conversations and absent in our discussions within teacher education. In this group of essays, the authors convey critiques of our current benumbed condition and attempt to remedy that condition by "filling in the gaps." Rarely in the educational literature do I hear or read about the conceptions they explore. It is not often that I come across elaborations of the tragic nature of the educational relationship, the role of irony and the illumination of the soul in our educational lives, the development of style in pedagogy, or the importance of hospitality in our educational institutions. The authors have accomplished a remarkable feat. They have not only enlisted critiques of our "technological" age, but they have also offered thoughtful and sensitive elaborations to redirect our educational focus.

Unfortunately, we live in an age in which there are not only numerous gaps in the educational conversation, but there are also immense holes in the institutional structure of teacher education. Our schools of education frequently do not serve well the teacher education enterprise. All too often the tasks and chores of teacher education are belittled, disregarded, and ignored.[1] Even though teacher education constitutes the basic function of institutional life (that is for schools, colleges, and departments of education), few scholars within our schools of education call themselves teacher educators. In our schools of education the chores and tasks of teacher education are viewed as the institutional drudge work—somewhat akin to the necessary but denigrated domestic labor of our home lives. In fact, it seems that teacher education has become the domestic labor of our institutional lives.[2] It is the essential yet essentially devalued work that reproduces

129

and sustains our schools of education. Within the institutional structure of our schools of education and our teacher education programs, the gaps and failings are many. Until we examine not only the "intellectual" gaps in our educational conversation, but also the institutional gaps of our schools of education, I fear that the wisdom conveyed in the preceding pages will fall between those institutional cracks. We have to find ways for the kinds of discussions contained in this book to become a presence in teacher education, to inform prospective and practicing teachers, and to engage those who toil in departments, schools, and colleges of education. And in order to do that we need for scholars of all stripes and persuasions to take part in the teacher education endeavor.

For my contribution to this collection of essays I have been asked to comment on themes elaborated in these essays and to place the themes within a context of teacher education. I will do that and then highlight features of our institutional (university) lives that encourage us to ignore or diminish the importance of teacher education.

Intellectual Gaps

During the last two decades educational writers have criticized our societal fetish for technological fixes. In this volume the authors continue that tradition and, in doing so, call to mind Ray Callahan's (1962) path-breaking work, *Education and the Cult of Efficiency*. In that work Callahan documented the historical development of the social efficiency movement, highlighting its focus on social control and institutional efficiency. However, in contrast to Callahan's work, the value of this collection lies not so much in the criticism leveled but rather in the ideals and sentiments articulated.

The authors present ideals that appear reasonable and attractive. In an age that overlooks what is essentially human in all of us, these authors demand that we pause to examine that humanity and to embrace its strengths and weaknesses. Many of the authors place teachers and students at the center of the educational enterprise and they ask us to treat this endeavor with care and attention. They invite us to become more fully human. Within this context many of the contributors view the practice of teaching as a fragile and ambiguous endeavor, one that tends to elude our analysis. In spite of this elusive sense, the authors capably "capture" certain features of the educational endeavor and offer these features up for our inspection. I would like to underscore just a few of those reflections and analyses, and examine them in light of the teacher education endeavor. I will not comment on each piece, but I will underline concepts that seem central to a vision that I share with a few of the authors—one rooted in a conception of care for and attention to others.[3]

In recent work both Nel Noddings (1984; 1987) and Jane Roland Martin (1992; 1994) have highlighted the concepts of care, connection, and concern. Noddings has been influential in bringing to light an ethic of care in the classroom, and Martin has enlarged the educational terrain to incorporate what she has called the three C's. Both Noddings and Martin have brought to the educational discussion a consideration of virtues, practices, and dispositions that have been previously ignored. In many ways their work is an attempt to elaborate rich and alternative conceptions of the way teachers and students attend to one another. In doing so they have offered conceptions of "the good" educational life. Another writer, philosopher and novelist Iris Murdoch (1971) has articulated a related conception of "the good," one that construes our moral (and I would add educational) relations with others as fairly complex, one that depends on our "attending" to, and focusing on, the other individuals involved. Lawrence Blum has characterized Murdoch's approach as a viewpoint which maintains that:

> . . .achieving knowledge of the particular other person toward whom one acts is an often complex and difficult moral task, and one which draws on specifically moral capacities. Understanding the needs, interests, and welfare of another person, and understanding the relationship between oneself and that other, requires a stance toward that person informed by care, love, empathy, compassion, and emotional sensitivity. It involves, for example, the ability to see the other as different in important ways from oneself, as a being existing in her own right, rather than viewing her through a simple projection of what one would feel if one were in her situation. (Blum, 1993, p. 51)

Murdoch examines this type of moral relationship at length in her work *The Sovereignty of Good* (1971). She portrays features of it by describing the way in which a mother (M) alters her original and negative opinions about her daughter-in-law (D).[4] As Murdoch relates, M initially construed her daughter-in-law as rude, brusque, and tirelessly juvenile. M then reflects on the situation and gives "careful and just attention" to both her relationship with D and her own attitudes. Upon reflection M realizes that she may be old fashioned, conventional, snobbish, and narrow-minded in her approach. She knows she is jealous. Subsequently, M comes to a different appraisal.

She sees D as no longer vulgar but "refreshingly simple, not undignified but spontaneous, not noisy but gay, not tiresomely juvenile but delightfully youthful, and so on" (Murdoch, 1971, pp. 17–18). Murdoch writes that such an attainment is neither simple nor uncomplicated, and is the result of being moved by love and justice. Murdoch maintains that such achievements are made quite difficult by our "humanness." She writes:

> Human beings are far more complicated and enigmatic and ambiguous than languages or mathematical concepts, and selfishness operates in a much more devious and frenzied manner in our relations with them. Ignorance, muddle, fear, wishful thinking, lack of tests often make us feel that moral choice is something arbitrary, a matter for personal will rather than for attentive study. Our attachments tend to be selfish and strong, and the transformation of our loves from selfishness to unselfishness is sometimes hard even to conceive of. Yet is the situation really so different? Should a retarded child be kept at home or sent to an institution? Should an elderly relation who is a trouble-maker be cared for or asked to go away? Should an unhappy marriage be continued for the sake of the children? Should I neglect them in order to practice my art? The love which brings the right answer is an exercise of justice and realism and really **looking**. The difficulty is to keep the attention fixed upon the real situation and to prevent it from returning surreptitiously to the self with consolations of self-pity, resentment, fantasy, and despair. . . . Of course virtue is good habit and dutiful action. But the background condition of such habit and action, in human beings, is just a mode of vision and a good quality of consciousness. It is a **task** to come to see the world as it is. (Murdoch, 1971, p. 91)

Murdoch's "attentive gaze" has much in common with certain themes elaborated in the present work, themes that are central, I believe, to a more robust and morally sound teacher education enterprise. The conceptions of hospitality, openness, and dialogue seem to fuse with and further inform Iris Murdoch's concern for "attention" in our relationship with others. This is a very rich set of issues and ones that do not now find comfortable homes in our schools of education.

Consider hospitality. Hospitality demands, writes Rud, that we listen first to ourselves and then to others. In teaching, Rud writes that this requires a "mindfulness" toward children and an attention to "ourselves" as teachers. It means, as Rud (quoting Nouwen, 1975) states:

...primarily the creation of a free space where the stranger can enter and become a friend instead of an enemy. Hospitality is not to change people, but to offer them space where change can take place...Teaching, therefore, asks first of all the creation of a space where students and teachers can enter into fearless communication with each other and allow their respective life experiences to be their primary and most valuable source of growth and experience. (Nouwen, 1975, pp. 71, 85, 87)

In an era in which hospitality tends to be viewed as unimportant, Rud breathes greater life back into the concept. He conveys a sense of invitation and communication that beckons to embrace and transform its recipients. He portrays hospitality as an essential engagement with and attention to students.

While certainly ennobling and enriching, Rud's conception of hospitality in teaching is also oddly depressing. It becomes depressing when I compare the goal with the reality of everyday interactions. For as much as I hear talk about the importance of students at the university and within schools of education, rarely are they viewed as beings with whom we ought to engage. Instead, universities tend to "put students up for the night," in a setting that neither engages their minds nor arouses their passions, in the hopes that they will move on after their stay. Rarely do we find schools of education and teacher education programs embracing, communicating with, transforming, or engaging its students. Seldom do we create hospitable environments.

Universities, especially research institutions, place a much greater emphasis and value on research than teaching. Faculty in schools, colleges, and departments of education, are rewarded for their research efforts and expected to teach. The modern multi-versity has become a collection of research entrepreneurs who tend to "put up" with rather than engage in teaching. When faculty are recognized for teaching it is frequently the result of a teaching excellence award, and as such, has the feel of a winning lotto ticket rather than a rigorous examination of one's teaching. Teaching is simply not taken seriously by many within the institution.

But it seems that schools of education, for their very survival, had better attend to what it means to create a hospitable teaching and learning environment. With fewer and fewer resources, state budgets will shrink and legislators will look for ways to downsize the university structure. Experienced teachers are likely not to come back to settings that treat them poorly. It is time for those in schools of education to listen. For the professional development of experienced teachers a hospitable environment would seem to demand that schools of education listen and attend to the experiences of elementary and secondary teachers. If experienced professionals could "enter into fearless communication with each other and allow their respective life experiences to be their primary and most valuable source of growth and experience" (Nouwen, 1975, p. 85) the professional development would be rooted and grounded in a way that honors and respects the teachers. Such an approach to professional development would, I sense, alter the dynamics between school practitioners and university faculty and researchers. It would, I believe, require that the professoriate educate themselves. It would, I think, be an enhanced and improved course of professional development.

In other essays concerns for dialogue and openness are developed in ways that seem quite compatible with Rud's idea of hospitality, and Murdoch's concern for attention towards others. In chapter 6, Leonard Waks develops an idea of emptiness, a "radical openness to reality," and he enjoins us to engage the world with compassionate intellect. His observations on Socrates, Jesus, and Gautama highlight the irreducibly human features of our shared existence and call for a radical self openness to face and accept others. He notes that:

> ...there is nothing in others which is *fundamentally* other, nothing in others which they might experience in themselves. In their humanness, they and others are one. Thus emptiness is the standpoint not merely for profound intellectual penetration of reality, but also for compassion and unconditional love. (Waks, p. 95)

Compassion and unconditional love are certainly laudable goals. It would seem that prospective and practicing teachers could be encouraged to recognize those times when their own defenses and prejudices arise to interfere with a mindfulness toward students and fellow teachers.

In education we have our own contemporary and perhaps less formidable teachers to emulate. While Vivian Paley (1981; 1989) does not rank "up there" with Socrates or Jesus, I sense that her classroom interactions and reflections are guided by this disposition of radical openness. For it is in work such as *White Teacher* (and others) that she shows how she is open to others, and in doing so, she explores her fears and her longings. Her reflections are honest and vulnerable, and underscore her attempt to come to terms with her attitudes about race, culture, and teaching. But rarely do we, at the university, engage in classroom dialogues that recognize our own fears and misunderstandings. Paley's reflections are rare treats for she shares with us her own insecurities, and as a result, we glimpse our own fears and defenses.

In an era in which future teachers must learn to bridge the gaps between distinct cultural worlds, where vast differences exist among students and between students and teachers, a concern for radical openness is certainly a valuable orientation. We tend not to walk around with a radical openness towards others but rather with an ever present defensiveness. First-year teachers, overwhelmed by the tasks they confront and the complexity of the endeavor, are frequently intimidated. All too often they rely on seclusion, exclusion, and threats. The effect of such a defensive posture is the elimination of possibilities and a sense of false, and always tentative, security. Experienced teachers learn ways to manage their lives and classrooms and, in effect, frequently close themselves off to features of reality.

In contrast, a sense of openness bespeaks an ability to see in each of us the humanity that we share. This is not a simple accomplishment, especially in an era in which difference is either so blindly celebrated or absolutely denigrated. Certainly we need to recognize that differences of all sorts exist, and that power differentials attend societally sanctioned distinctions. An understanding of our shared humanity does not have to ignore the alienation that results from these power differentials. Instead it seems that a sense of openness demands that schools of education attend to our shared human features and engage in analyses of power, culture, class, race, and gender that illuminate the manner in which these differences might harm others.

Sophie Haroutunian-Gordon highlights and examines the meaning of the soul and dialogue for today's educational discussion. In doing so, she emphasizes the ambiguity inherent in the meaning of the soul, the texts we read, and the student-teacher relationship. For Haroutunian-Gordon an individual's "soul" both illuminates and is illuminated in its quest for the truth. The soul both provides and receives illumination. For Haroutunian-Gordon this same interaction is present in learning. She illustrates this when she turns to a high school discussion of *Romeo and Juliet*. Commenting on that discussion she states:

> This text, focusing as it does on adolescent love, draws out of these adolescent readers beliefs about the effects of love—beliefs they may never have articulated before. The text, then, seems both to illuminate those beliefs—to shed light upon them— and to itself be illuminated by them. (p. 101)

For Haroutunian-Gordon, the text highlights this interaction and points to an important lesson that we ought not forget:

> The presence of the ambiguity should prompt us to ask not how to insert vision into blind eyes, or even draw out the vision that the soul possesses, but rather how to provide experience that re-directs everyone's vision. Plato's suggestion for doing so can be summarized in one word: dialogue. (p. 103)

In teacher education we could engage more in this sort of dialogue. We could provide experiences that redirect students' and instructors' visions. This would require texts, experiences, and instructional approaches akin to Haroutunian-Gordon's example of the dialogue focused on *Romeo and Juliet*. It would be a dialogue that draws out of prospective and practicing teachers their beliefs about teaching, invites them to be open and hospitable towards themselves and others, searches and enriches their memories of past educational relationships, has them consider existing and alternative conceptions of teacher authority, and asks them to articulate and justify proposed educational actions. But this sort of dialogue is difficult to find and arduous to create. It requires that teaching and the focus on teaching become central features of schools of education and their teacher education programs. While this is certainly feasible in some institutions, and within some teacher education programs, it certainly goes against the established institutional grain. Research, not teaching, teacher education, or educational program development, constitutes the focus for careers in higher education. Dialogue is not a valued aim.

In the bare presentation that I have offered thus far, Rud's understanding of hospitality, Waks's sense of openness, and Haroutunian-Gordon's conception of dialogue seem to fit well with Murdoch's concern for careful and just attention. Taken together, they begin to form a conception of instruction that highlights the ambiguity of educational conceptions and practices, underscores the complexity and intricacies of those practices and conceptions, and emphasizes the need to balance, integrate, and overcome our reliance on educational dualisms. Taken together, they point me in a direction that demands I pay much greater attention to those with whom I interact and to myself. Taken together, they orient me toward educational relationships that are guided by an enhanced understanding of the "other," by a value for the other, and by a critical understanding of my relation to the other. Taken together, they bring to me a radically different way of construing education and schooling.

However, the obstacles and the problems entailed in acting on these understandings are many. In an endeavor that shines light on goals that ought to be attained, it seems reasonable to underscore the aphorism "ought implies can." When we urge ourselves and others to redirect our vision, our understanding, our gaze—we are demanding that we see and act differently. My "realist" inclinations demand that such a redirection take into account the institutional obstacles that would tend to swallow up such an endeavor. Hospitality, radical openness, and dialogue do not find comfortable homes in our schools, colleges, and departments of education. And for these views to ever find a home in teacher education, the denigration of teacher education in our schools of education needs to be acknowledged and altered. In order for these conceptions to enliven teacher education—the tasks, the chores, and the demands of teacher education must be embraced, not belittled. For too long teacher education has functioned as the domestic labor of our institutional lives with much of the effort being relegated to "others." Whether one is a philosopher, educational psychologist, or a sociologist the desire and the institutional message is clear: "flee teacher education," it will not help your career. It seems indeed difficult to envision any alteration in the education of teachers until this message is altered.

Institutional Obstacles

Teaching Teachers

In the previous section I drew on the work of others to articulate a view of teacher education, one that would entail a greater engagement with, and further involvement in, our prospective and practicing teachers' education. The implication of this call is that we need to spend more time and exert greater energies in our efforts to educate teachers. However, given the nature of institutionalized teacher education, I fear that such a call may carry with it negative, albeit unintentional, consequences. It may be akin to asking a mother of twelve children to parent harder and better while "unloading" six foster children at her back door. Certainly this is not the intent. A description of the teacher education terrain should give us a better idea of some of the likely consequences of pursuing these goals. With the likely consequences identified, the goals may seem difficult to achieve. Unfortunately, it may be that a more hospitable and engaging approach is simply not feasible within our current institutional constraints.

Teaching prospective teachers is not an easy task; it is avoided, belittled, and when performed, it is usually done so begrudgingly. It is a messy ordeal, one that can be difficult to control or predict—at times emotionally trying and intense. Teaching teachers generally entails larger classes and a younger, less sophisticated student population. In teacher education courses questions of practice and preparation loom large: cognitive dissonance and affective apprehensions surface and both craft-based and research-oriented matters arise. The university, especially the research oriented school of education, deals best with questions of practice when they are contained and intellectualized. Students, however, fueled by the fears and apprehensions that animate their lives, cannot always mold their concerns to fit the research paradigms. There is a problem of fit. The conundrums of the craft of teaching, whether they be moral or practical, occupy some prospective teachers and loom large as issues in the profession. Standard research, however, has little to say about those matters. In teacher education, training and reflection are required: they are required in a manner that recognizes the place and importance of each component. In the preparation of teachers there are issues to examine, skills and behaviors to develop, and norms and values to inspect. Research can contribute, but it is certainly not the only, nor perhaps the central component in the preparation of teachers.

In teacher education there is a preferred trinity of program components. Generally students are given instructional methods, social and psychological foundations, and field experience (e.g. student teaching) courses. These three types of educational experiences constitute the backbone of teacher education in the United States. In the "methods" component, instructors generally feel compelled to "train" students in a particular pedagogical approach or to acquaint students with a range of pedagogical strategies employed in that content area. Generally these skills or approaches conflict, or simply do not coincide, with the practices found in the local schools. The university teaches one approach while the local school district adheres to another. The university faculty tend to teach the "proper" approach and view teachers in the local school district as simply not able to put it into practice. Students see the disjuncture and, in the end, they go with the established, institutional elementary and secondary practices. In the foundations course work the disciplinary content (e.g. psychology, sociology, and philosophy) often seems removed and remote from the every day travails of schools and students. Knowledge and discipline-based problems rather than felt and perceived issues seem to animate the discussion. For many students the disciplinary "solutions" seem to be empty and unsatisfactory. In the end, students sense that foundation course work provides little in the way of any sort of foundational understanding and seems to be simply one more set of courses to take and get out of the way. Student teaching is the pinnacle of the teacher education experience and it usually begins the true education/socialization of the teacher. This "capstone" experience tends to reject, rather than utilize, large portions of what went on before it.[5]

For faculty members in teacher education the levels of uncertainty and ambiguity are generally high and the rewards fairly low. Talking about teaching practice when one's experience tends to be dated (or non-existent) is not the most comfortable or secure setting for instruction. Teacher education is a labor intensive endeavor, one that requires attention to the students, the existing literature, the local schools, and the university's program. Students' excitement and apprehensions, the research literature's inability to address directly questions of practice, the normally tenuous relationship with the local schools, and the bureaucratic university and state requirements can be taxing and are certainly time consuming and labor intensive. Chores, minute and large, abound and range from addressing a student's personal needs to wending one's way through the current state legislation and local bureaucracy.

At the university the production of research is the most highly valued endeavor with teaching and service counting for very little. Time spent in the labor intensive area of teacher education is lost and not to be recovered for the research effort. One learns to leave these endeavors behind, to limit one's interactions with prospective teachers, and to restrict both the range of issues discussed and the time available in interactions with prospective teachers. One learns that while such tasks constitute some of the central functions of a school of education, they are neither recognized nor rewarded.

Teacher Education and Domestic Labor

And so when I read, endorse, and formulate calls to educate prospective teachers in a more hospitable, radically open, dialogical fashion, I fear that such calls cannot become a reality given the current state of teacher education. I fear that such calls will not be shared by the entire faculty of a school of education but will become, at most, the domain of a small group of overworked and relatively unrecognized teacher educators. If one stood before a school of education and asked the faculty how many are active in and considered themselves to be teacher educators— it is doubtful that many would rise. When I travel around the country Deans and Chairs frequently tell me that in their school it is only one segment of the faculty that carries the teacher education load. Frequently this group is the faculty within the division of Curriculum and Instruction. And so it seems that in our calls to become more hospitable, more open, and more adept at enhancing our educational dialogues we ought to understand whom we are asking to do what and how much we are asking them to do. If "ought implies can" we need to attend to the way our educational labor is structured in our schools of education. If we do not attend to the structure of our work lives, it seems likely that calls for reform will not take hold.

When one examines the structure of work in schools of education, it seems that teacher education constitutes the domestic labor of that institutional setting. Let me explain further the analogy. In any and every home someone performs the domestic labor. Domestic labor entails the necessary, ongoing, and time-intensive (reproductive) tasks of "keeping house." It frequently includes the work that accompanies raising children, and it has traditionally been performed by women rather than men. It is the recursive, time-intensive, and frequently emotional labor that reproduces the basis for our daily lives. It is never ending and emotionally taxing. Domestic labor includes the daily chores of cooking, cleaning (clothes, utensils, and living quarters) and, when children are present, caring for children. Caring for children entails clothing, feeding, educating, and loving them. In effect, domestic labor is non-waged work that is traditionally performed by women; provides the necessary basics for, and thus reproduces, daily life in the home setting; benefits others, and frequently entails a high degree of emotional involvement. It is low status, intensive work for which little recognition is given.[6] Let me take some of these points and point to the parallels within teacher education.

Domestic labor is non-waged work that is performed in the home. It is not paid for directly. Similarly one could argue that involvement in teacher education programs constitutes work that is performed in schools of education, but which in a very real sense, is also non-waged work. In schools of education, especially research-based schools, faculty are expected to teach and do "some" service. However, neither teaching nor service are critically assessed. They rarely constitute the basis upon which people are hired, fired (except for egregious errors of judgment), promoted, or financially rewarded. Research is the single most important element and it constitutes the basis for the wage labor in research institutions. The parallel can be seen in another way. Imagine the effort required for a teacher education endeavor to become a "program." For teacher education endeavors to become more than a collection of state and tradition mandated courses, it is necessary for faculty to collaborate and plan course work and field experiences. Faculty would need to plan collaboratively and work together with other university and public school personnel. Generally, faculty find it much easier to stick to their state mandated and tradition bound courses and to teach and plan alone rather than together. The extra work required in collaborative efforts is not seen as rewarded, professionally or monetarily, by the institution. The extra effort, if performed, would simply be non-waged labor—either "forced" labor or a labor of love.

Domestic labor is also low status work, for which little recognition is given and which generally benefits others. For many individuals, work around the home is considered a necessary evil, part of our "private lives." It certainly benefits those within the home who eat the meals, wear the clothes, and grow from the nourishment and care that is provided. Those who work in teacher education programs probably recognize that their status is low in the institutional scheme of things. In research institutions they are frequently adjuncts hired on for part-time work or teachers who envision a better life at the university. Their work benefits those who engage in research education and the research projects unrelated to the tasks of teacher education. Teacher education provides the home base from which educational researchers can ply their trade. Teacher educators create the institutional rubric from which researchers work. But while this fact sustains the institutions, while it is the teacher education enterprise that provides the justification for the institution's existence, rarely is this work recognized and allotted the material and monetary benefits it deserves. Rarely is a professor recognized, embraced, and rewarded for work in teacher education.

Domestic labor, when it is focused on a spouse or children, entails a significant degree of emotional engagement and investment. Caring for others takes a considerable amount of personal attention and energy. Teaching well, no matter what level—elementary, secondary, and tertiary—is labor intensive. Teaching children well requires a great deal of emotional investment. It entails working through one's own and on others' emotions in order to motivate and engage children in learning. Teaching prospective teachers to teach children entails a similar investment of emotion.

Conclusion

There are other parallels between teacher education and domestic labor but what has passed should suffice. If we are going to call for distinct visions to guide our teacher education endeavors then we need to pay heed to the realities of teacher education. Without a degree of attention to those realities I fear that teacher education will remain the essential and the essentially disregarded work in our schools of education. Without some attention to what is, our moral claims become empty calls for enhanced directions. The essays presented in this collection deserve much more. They promise much more.

Notes

Chapter 1 Introduction

1. Labaree goes on to note that in the 1990 report of The Holmes Group titled *Tomorrow's Schools* "these two themes—citizenship and collaboration—provide the basic rhetorical structure..." (pp. 633–634). Still, Labaree concludes, "it is misleading because both the substance and the agents of reform reflect a politics directly at odds with democratic values." As he sees it the latter report is just disciplinary technology by subtler means.

2. Many of the contributors to our book, along with others that we mention, will refer to Robert Bellah and colleagues (1985) and their desire "to deepen our understanding of the resources our tradition provides—and fails to provide—for enabling us to think about the kinds of moral problems we are currently facing as Americans. We also hope to make articulate the all-too-inarticulate search of those we have described...to find a moral language..." (p. 21; cf. Coles, 1989). In their preface Bellah and colleagues observe that "...people...often live in ways they cannot put into words. It is particularly here, in the tension between how we live and what our culture allows us to say, that we have found both some of our richest insights into the dilemmas our society faces and hope for the reappropriation of a common language in which those dilemmas can be discussed" (p. vii). Our goal in the present volume is the more modest one of exploring the tensions created in the gaps between how we "live" as teachers and teacher educators that we are not allowed to say in the legitimated culture of scientistic discourse so influential in second wave educational reform.

3. Sockett, like so many others who discuss the absence of a moral dimension in American life, is referring to the work of Robert Bellah and colleagues (1985).

Chapter 3 Authority and the Tragic Dimension of Teaching

1. In this essay, my arguments are only directed toward problems of authority in teaching. There are many other related problems of authority, especially the question of political authority, to which I will not refer. It may be, however, that some of my arguments here pertain to those other contexts.

2. Many of the insights in this paragraph arose in conversations with Suzanne Rice.

Chapter 5 Pragmatism and the Ironic Teacher of Virtue

1. Richard Rorty is a pragmatic philosopher who has announced "the end of Philosophy" (capital P), by which he means we should abandon the search for timeless Truths, indubitable logic, eternal essences, or any foundations of knowledge (epistemology) and existence (metaphysics) that transcend contingent human experience.

2. Rorty's most sustained discussion of irony is to be found in Rorty (1989), pp. 73–78. To a large extent, I am, in this and my next few paragraphs, glossing his view as stated here. Comments by Vaughn McKim and Karl Hostetler on my "Ironic Schooling" paper encouraged me to be clearer, in this section, about how pragmatic irony is not merely fallibilism.

3. O'Connor uses this language in an unpublished essay review of Gregory Vlastos' *Socrates: Ironist and Moral Philosopher* entitled "Constructing Vlastos' Socrates." A good statement by James of the radical empiricist point of view can be found in the preface to his *The Will to Believe* (1956), where he says: "For him (the radical empiricist) the crudity of experience remains an eternal element thereof. There is no possible point of view from which the world can appear an absolutely single fact."

4. Assuming that we do not "ossify" the practical division in parts into a metaphysical divide.

5. Milan Kundera became a censored author, unable to publish and earn a living from his work after the Russian invasion of Czechoslovakia in 1968. Some see his books as an ironic parody of the literal Truth foisted upon his nation by an army of occupation.

6. Milan Kundera, (1987). Over the course of the last three summers I have taught this novel along with the *Symposium* with my friend and colleague, Basil O'Leary. I find it hard to separate out what is his and what is mine in the discussion here of these texts, but I know that Professor O'Leary's insights have been crucial to my thinking. At certain points, such as the very idea of Sabina as Saint, I can pinpoint O'Leary's originality. In general, however, I simply want to thank him and hope that I haven't done a terrible injustice to his careful thinking.

7. In these comments I am indebted to two papers: Terence Martin's unpublished "When the Dead Speak: Serio-Comic Dialogue and Religious Discourse" and René Arcilla's (1991) "Metaphysics in Education after Hutchins and Dewey." My reference to William James points ultimately, of course, to his masterful and indispensable *Varieties of Religious Experience: A Study in Human Nature* (1936). For my understanding of James on experience, I am indebted to Bruce W. Wilshire, in his introduction to a collection he edited, *William James: The Essential Writings* (1984).

8. See Richard Schacht, (1980).

Chapter 7 Soul

1. The advent of modern psychology is frequently associated with Wilhelm Wundt, who set up the first experimental psychology laboratory in Leipzig in 1875. Among other works, he authored volumes on psychological theory that were translated by E. B. Titchener as *Principles of Physiological Psychology* in 1904. His theories, as well as those of William James and others, did much to establish the modern concept of the "psyche," whose development became the preoccupation to which the science of psychology is devoted. Modern educational theories have been constructed upon the stories provided by modern psychological theory. See Leonard Waks's discussion of "psyche" in chapter 6.

2. All Plato citations are taken from *The Collected Dialogues of Plato* (1961). Hamilton, E. & Cairns, H. (Eds.) Princeton: Princeton University Press.

3. Among many references see *Meno*, lines 77–78; *Protagoras*, lines 345D, 358C-D; *Philebus*, 22B; *Sophist*, 230A; *Laws*, 734B, 860D. In *Laws*, 731C Plato wrote:

> . . .we must first of all rest assured that no wrongdoer is so of deliberation. For no man will ever deliberately admit supreme evil, and least of all in his most precious possessions. But every man's most precious possession, as we said, is his soul; no man then, we may be sure, will of set purpose receive the supreme evil into this most precious thing and live with it there all his life through. And yet, though a wrongdoer or a man in evil case is always a pitiable creature, it is with him whose disease is curable that there is scope for pity.

4. The Master of Science Program in Education and Social Policy at Northwestern University, which I direct, prepares people with liberal arts degrees to become elementary or secondary teachers. Each student pursues a Master's Project, which is developed over the duration of the program, and which provides the student with opportunity to cultivate a personal interest in depth. The projects have involved art, music, drama, literature, history, science, educational issues, film, and video work. These projects frequently, although not always, tie directly into classroom activities.

Chapter 8 *Some Thoughts on Privacy in Classrooms*

1. Dewey presented this position as early as *The School and Society* in 1900, and as late as *Experience and Education* in 1925. In between, it was central to his argument in *Democracy and Education* in 1916.

2. The student shall remain nameless, in respect of her privacy; she wrote a paper on the topic and this quotation comes directly from it, although describing a "fictional" child named Betsy.

3. There is an exception: the teacher who is dealing with a badly crippled student who cannot respond. The teacher's actions—frustrating to say the least—will not be rewarded by the usual sort of interaction, but we still might say that she/he is teaching her/his student. There are also borderline cases: the lecturer with a class of five hundred students is one. Undoubtedly there are others.

4. A good beginning on the study of virtues in education is Pincoffs (1986).

Chapter 9 *Learning in Comfort: Developing an Ethos of Hospitality in Education*

1. The preliminary work of making oneself ready to welcome others is a necessary condition for the conception of hospitality developed here. William Losito (1992) presents a fine and sensitive discussion of hospitality in Homer and in the Bible. He argues well for making room for hospitality and other little-used metaphors in education. Yet Losito does not focus on the preliminary work of being at home with oneself that lies at the core of my interpretation of the Benedictines, Thoreau, Nouwen, Palmer, and my own work in teacher renewal (cf. Rud, 1992; also *Mark* 12:31 "You must love your neighbor as yourself," cited in Nouwen, 1975, p. 81).

2. I want to thank Rita Rud, Dan Fredricks, Jim Garrison, Mike Jones, Mark Packer, and members of the NCCAT seminar "On Ancient and Contemporary Hospitality," especially its leader, Carolyn Toben, for comments and conversation as I wrote this chapter.

Chapter 10 *Intellectual and Institutional Gaps in Teacher Education*

1. See, for example, Clifford and Guthrie (1988) and Goodlad (1990).

2. For a more extended analysis see Liston, "Work in Teacher Education: A Current Assessment of U.S. Teacher Education," (forthcoming).

3. An earlier but only initial attempt along these lines can be found in Liston and Zeichner (1987).

4. See Murdoch (1971) pp. 17-24.

5. See Zeichner and Gore (1990).

6. For a succinct bibliography of the domestic labor literature see MacKinnon (1989).

Bibliography

Arcilla, R. V. (1991). Metaphysics in education after Hutchins and Dewey. *Teachers College Record,* (93)2, 280–289.

Arcilla, R. V. (1992). Tragic absolutism in education. *Educational Theory,* 42(4), 473–481.

Bellah, R. N., Madsen, R., Sullivan, W. M., Swidler, A., & Tipton, S. M. (1985). *Habits of the heart: Individualism and commitment in American life.* New York: Harper & Row.

Benne, K. (1986). The locus of educational authority in today's world. *Teachers College Record, 88*(1), 15–21.

Bernstein, R. J. (1983). *Beyond objectivism and relativism: Science, hermeneutics, and practice.* Philadelphia: University of Pennsylvania Press.

Bernstein, R. J. (1990). Rorty's liberal utopia. *Social Research, 57*(1), 30–72.

Bloom, A. (1987). *The closing of the American mind.* New York: Simon and Schuster, Inc.

Blum, L. (1993). Gilligan and Kohlberg: Implications for moral theory. In *An Ethic of Care* 49–68. Mary Jeanne Larrabee (Ed.) New York: Routledge.

Bobbitt, F. (1913). *The supervision of city schools: Some general principles of management applied to the problems of city-school systems.* Twelfth Yearbook of the National Society for the Study of Education, Part 1. Bloomington, IN: NSSE.

Bottomore, T. B. (1963). *Karl Marx: Early writings.* New York: McGraw-Hill.

Buber, M. (1955). *Between man and man* (trans. R. G. Smith). Boston: Beacon Press.

Buber, M. (1970). *I and thou* (trans. W. Kaufmann). New York: Charles Scribner's Sons.

Burbules, N. C. (1986). Radical educational cynicism and radical educational skepticism. In D. Nyberg (Ed.), *Philosophy of Education 1985,* 201–205, Normal: Philosophy of Education Society.

Burbules, N. C. (1990). The tragic sense of education. *Teachers College Record, 91*(4), 468–479.

Burbules, N. C. (1993). *Dialogue in teaching: Theory and practice.* New York: Teachers College Press.

Burbules, N. C. & Densmore, K. (1991a). The limits of making teaching a profession. *Educational Policy, 5*(1), 44–63.

Burbules, N. C. & Densmore, K. (1991b). The persistence of professionalism: Breakin' up is hard to do. *Educational Policy, 5*(2), 150–157.

Burbules, N. C. & Rice, S. (1991). Dialogue across differences: Continuing the conversation. *Harvard Educational Review, 61*(4), 393–416.

Burbules, N. C. & Rice, S. (1992). Can we be heard? *Harvard Educational Review, 62*(2), 264–271.

Burnett, J. (1968). The Socratic doctrine of the soul. *Essays and Addresses.* (126–162). Freeport: Books for Libraries Press, Essay Index Reprint Series. (Original work published in 1930).

Callahan, R. (1962). *Education and the cult of efficiency.* Chicago: University of Chicago Press.

Camus, A. (1969). The myth of Sisyphus. In *The Myth of Sisyphus and Other Essays,* 119–123. New York: Knopf.

Carnegie Task Force on Teaching as a Profession (1986). *A nation prepared: Teachers for the 21st century.* New York: Carnegie Corporation.

Cavell, S. (1974). *The senses of Walden.* New York: Viking.

Clifford, G. J. & Guthrie, J. W. (1988). *Ed school.* Chicago: University of Chicago Press.

Coles, R. (1989). *The call of stories: Teaching and the moral imagination.* Boston: Houghton Mifflin.

Colledge, E. & McGinn, B. (1981). *Meister Eckhart.* New York: Paulist Press.

Dewey, J. (1916). *Democracy and education.* New York: Macmillan.

Dewey, J. (1916a; 1980). Democracy and education. In Jo Ann Boydston (Ed.), *John Dewey: The Middle Works, 1899–1924, Volume 9.* Carbondale and Edwardsville: Southern Illinois University Press.

Dewey, J. (1916b; 1980). Force and coercion. In Jo Ann Boydston (Ed.), *John Dewey: The Middle Works, 1899–1924, Volume 10.* 244–251. Carbondale and Edwardsville: Southern Illinois University Press.

Dewey, J. (1925; 1981). Experience and nature. In Jo Ann Boydston (Ed.), *John Dewey: The Later Works, 1925–1953, Volume 1.* Carbondale and Edwardsville: Southern Illinois University Press.

Dewey, J. (1927; 1984). The Public and its problems. In Jo Ann Boydston (Ed.), *John Dewey: The Later Works, 1925–1953, Volume 2,* 235–372. Carbondale and Edwardsville: Southern Illinois University Press.

Dewey, J. (1929; 1984). *The quest for certainty.* In Jo Ann Boydston, *John Dewey: The Later Works, 1925–1953, Volume 4.* Carbondale and Edwardsville: Southern Illinois University Press.

Dewey, J. and Tafts, J. H. (1932; 1985). Ethics. In Jo Ann Boydston (Ed.), *John Dewey: The Later Works, 1925–1953, Volume 7.* Carbondale and Edwardsville: Southern Illinois University Press.

Dewey, J. (1934; 1987). Art as experience. In Jo Ann Boydston (Ed.), *John Dewey: The Later Works, 1925–1953, Volume 10.* Carbondale and Edwardsville: Southern Illinois University Press.

Dewey, J. (1938). *Experience and education.* New York: Collier Macmillan.

Dewey, J. (1939; 1988). Creative democracy—The task before us. In Jo Ann Boydston (Ed.), *John Dewey: The Later Works, 1925–1953, Volume 14,* 224–230. Carbondale and Edwardsville: Southern Illinois University Press.

Dewey, J. (1946). Religion, science and philosophy. *Problems of Men,* 169–179. New York: Philosophical Library, Inc.

Dewey, J. (1922; 1983). *Human nature and conduct.* In Jo Ann Boydston (Ed.), *John Dewey: The Middle Works, 1899–1924, Volume 14.* Carbondale and Edwardsville: Southern Illinois University Press.

Dewey, John (1919; 1982). *Philosophy and democracy.* In Jo Ann Boydston (Eds.), *John Dewey: The Middle Works, 1899–1924, Volume 11.* Carbondale and Edwardsville: Southern Illinois University Press.

Dewey, J. (1902; 1990). *The child and the curriculum.* Chicago: University of Chicago Press.

Doyle, W. (1978). Paradigms for research on teacher effectiveness. In *Review of Research in Education.* Itasca: Peacock.

Dreyfus, H. L. & Rabinow, P. (1986). What is maturity? Habermas and Foucault on "what is enlightenment?" In David Couzens Hoy (Ed.), *Foucault: A Critical Reader.* 109–121. Oxford: Basil Blackwell.

Eagleton, T. (1987). Estrangement and Irony. *Salmagundi, 73,* 25–33.

Education Commission of the States (1986). *What's next? More leverage for teachers.* Denver: Author.

Ellsworth, E. (1989). Why doesn't this feel empowering? Working through the repressive myths of critical pedagogy. *Harvard Educational Review, 59*(3), 297–324.

Ericson, D. P. & Ellett, F. S. (1982). Interpretation, understanding and educational research. *Teachers College Record, 83,* 497–513.

Fenstermacher, G. D. (1989). On the value of detached technique for becoming an expert. In *Philosophy of Education: 1988,* 62–65. Normal: Philosophy of Education Society.

Foucault, M. (1979). *Discipline and punish: The birth of the prison.* New York: Vintage.

Foucault, M. (1980). *Prison talk.* In *Power/Knowledge,* 37–54. New York: Pantheon Books.

Foucault, M. (1980). *Power/knowledge: Selected interviews and other writings, 1972–1977.* New York: Pantheon Books.

Foucault, M. (1983). On the genealogy of ethics: An overview of work in progress. In *Michel Foucault: Beyond Structuralism and Hermeneutics,*

229–252, 2nd ed. Hubert Dreyfus and Paul Rabinow (Eds.). Chicago: University of Chicago Press.

Foucault, M. (1984). What is enlightenment? In P. Rabinow (Ed.), *The Foucault Reader,* 32–50. New York: Pantheon.

Foucault, M. (1988). On power. In *Politics, Philosophy, Culture: Selected Interviews and Other Writings, 1977–1984,* 96–109. New York: Routledge.

Freire, P. (1970). *Pedagogy of the oppressed.* New York: Seabury.

Friedenberg, E. Z. (1965). *Coming of age in America: Growth and acquiescence.* New York: Random House.

Fry, T. (Ed.) (1982). *The rule of St. Benedict in English.* Collegeville: The Liturgical Press.

Gage, N. L. (1963). Paradigms for research on teaching. In N. L. Gage (Ed.), *Handbook of Research on Teaching.* Chicago: Rand-McNally.

Gage, N. L. (1978). *The scientific basis of the art of teaching.* New York: Teachers College Press.

Gage, N. L. (1983). When does research on teaching yield duplications for practice? *The Elementary School Journal, 83,* 492–496.

Garrison, J. W. & Macmillan, C. J. B. (1984). A philosophical critique of process-product research on teaching. *Educational Theory, 40,* 255–274.

Giroux, H. (1986). Authority, intellectuals, and the politics of practical learning. *Teachers College Record, 88*(1), 22–40.

Goodlad, J. (1990). *Teachers for our nation's schools.* San Francisco: Jossey-Bass.

Goodlad, J., Soder, R., & Sirotnik, K. (Eds.). (1990). *The moral dimensions of teaching.* San Francisco: Jossey-Bass.

Greene, M. (1988). *The dialectic of freedom.* New York: Teachers College Press.

Haroutunian-Gordon, S. (1991). *Turning the soul: Teaching through conversation in the high school.* Chicago: University of Chicago Press.

Haroutunian-Gordon, S. (in press). The role of narrative in interpretive discussion. In McEwan, H. & Egan, K. (Eds.), *Perspectives on narrative and teaching.* New York: Teachers College Press.

Haynes, F. (1986). Curriculum, democracy, and evaluation. *Teachers College Record, 88*(1), 81–84.

Heidegger, M. (1977). Building, dwelling, thinking. In D. Krell (Ed.) *Martin Heidegger: Basic writings,* 319–339. New York: Harper & Row.

Hirsch, E. D. (1987). *Cultural literacy: What every American needs to know.* Boston: Houghton Mifflin.

Hugo, V. (1979). *Les Miserables* (abridged edition). New York: Dodd, Mead. (Original work published 1862).

Ignatieff, M. (1984). *The needs of strangers*. New York: Viking Penguin.

James, W. (1936). *The varieties of religious experience: A study in human nature*. New York: The Modern Library.

James, W. (1956). *The will to believe*. New York: Dover Publications.

James, W. (1981). *Pragmatism*. Indianapolis: Hackett Publishing Co.

Jaspers, K. (1962). *Socrates, Buddha, Confucius, Jesus: The paradigmatic individuals*. New York: Harcourt Brace.

Johansson, R. (1969). *The psychology of Nirvana*. Garden City: Doubleday.

Kundera, M. (1987). *The unbearable lightness of being*. New York: Harper & Row.

Kundera, M. (1988). *The art of the novel*. New York: Harper and Row.

Labaree, D. (1992). Doing good, doing science: The Holmes Group reports and the rhetorics of educational reform. *Teachers College Record, 93*(4), 628–640.

Lentricchia, F. (1988). The return of William James. In *Ariel and the Police*. Madison: The University of Wisconsin Press.

Linbeck, G. (1984). *The nature of doctrine, religion, and theology in a postliberal age*. Philadelphia: The Westminster Press.

Liston, D. (forthcoming). Work in teacher education: A current assessment of U.S. teacher education. In *Teacher Education in Industrialized Nations*. N. Shimahara & I. Holowinsky (Eds.) New York: Garland Publishing.

Liston, D. & Zeichner, K. (1987). Reflective teacher education and moral deliberation. *Journal of Teacher Education 38*(6), 2–8.

Lortie, D. C. (1975). *Schoolteacher: A sociological study*. Chicago: The University of Chicago Press.

Losito, W. (1992). Education as hospitality: The reclamation of cultural metaphor and narrative. In W. Strandberg (Ed.), *In other voices: Expanding the educational conversation: Proceedings of the thirty-sixth annual meeting of the south atlantic philosophy of education society, 62–69*. Richmond: SAPES.

MacIntyre, A. (1981). *After virtue*. Notre Dame: University of Notre Dame Press.

MacKinnon, C. (1989). *Toward a feminist theory of the state*. Cambridge: Harvard University Press.

Maclean, N. (1992). *Young men and fire*. Chicago: University of Chicago Press.

Macmillan, C. J. B. & Garrison, J. W. (1988). *A logical theory of teaching: Erotetics and intentionality*. Dordrecht: Kluwer Academic Publishers.

Macmillan, C. J. B. and Pendlebury, S. (1985). The Florida performance measuring system: A consideration. *Teachers College Recorcd, 87*, 67–78.

Martin, J. (1992). *Schoolhome*. Cambridge: Harvard University Press.

Martin, J. (1994). *Changing the educational landscape*. New York: Routledge.

McCloskey, G. N., Provenzo, E. F., Cohn, M. M., Kottkamp, R. B. (1991). Disincentives to teaching: Teacher reactions to legislated learning. *Educational Policy, 5*(3), 251–265.

McKinney, J. R. & Garrison, J. W. (1993). Connecting the thoughts of Foucault and Rousseau on the role of the teacher in modern technocratic American education. *Journal of Thought, 28*(1 and 2), 61–82.

Murdoch, I. (1971). *The sovereignty of good*. New York: Schocken.

Nagel, T. (1979). Moral luck. In T. Nagel, *Mortal Questions*, 24–38. Cambridge: Cambridge University Press.

Nash, P. (1966). The authority of discipline. In *Authority and Freedom in Education*, 103–135. New York: Wiley.

National Commission on Excellence in Education (1983). *A nation at risk*. Washington, DC: Government Printing Office.

National Governor's Association (1986). *Time for results*. Washington, DC: Author.

Neiman, A. (1986). Education, power, and the authority of knowledge, *Teachers College Record, 88*(1), 64–80.

Neiman, A. (1991). Ironic schooling: Socrates, pragmatism, and the higher learning. *Educational Theory, 41*(4), 371–385.

Noddings, N. (1984). *Caring: A feminine approach to ethics and moral education*. Berkeley: University of California Press.

Noddings, N. (1987). Fidelity in teaching, teacher education and research for teaching. In *Teachers, teaching, and teacher education*, 384–400. M. Okazawa-Rey, J. Anderson, & R. Traver (Eds.) Cambridge: Harvard Educational Review (Reprint Series No. 19).

Noddings, N. (1992). *The challenge to care in schools: An alternative approach to education*. New York: Teachers College Press.

Nouwen, H. (1975). *Reaching out: The three movements of the spiritual life*. Garden City: Doubleday.

Nussbaum, M. C. (1986). *The fragility of goodness: Luck and ethics in Greek tragedy and philosophy*. Cambridge: Cambridge University Press.

Nussbaum, M. C. (1990). *Love's knowledge: Essays on philosophy and literature*. Oxford: Oxford University Press.

Nuyen, A. T. (1992). Lyotard on the death of the professor. *Educational Theory, 42*(1), 25–37.

Nyberg, D. & Farber, P. (1986). Authority in education. *Teachers College Record, 88*(1), 4–14.

Oakeshott, M. (1962). *Rationalism in politics*. New York: Basic Books.

O'Neil, J. (1992, October). On tracking and individual differences: A conversation with Jeannie Oakes. *Educational Leadership, 50*(2), 18–21.

Oxford English Dictionary, compact edition. (1971) Oxford: Oxford University Press.

Paley, V. (1981). *Wally's stories*. Cambridge: Harvard University Press.

Paley, V. (1989). *White teacher*. Cambridge: Harvard University Press.

Palmer, P. (1983). *To know as we are known: A spirituality of education*. San Francisco: Harper & Row.

Pendlebury, S. A. (1990). Practical reasoning and situational appreciation in teaching. *Educational Theory, 40*, 171–179.

Pendlebury, S. A. (1993). Practical arguments, rationalization and imagination in teachers' practical reasoning. *Journal of Curriculum Studies, 25*, 145–151.

Peters, R. S. (1966). Authority and education. In *Ethics and Education*, 237–265. Boston: George Allen and Unwin.

Pincoffs, E. L. (1986). *Quandaries and virtues: Against reductivism in ethics*. Lawrence: University Press of Kansas.

Purkey, W. & Novak, J. (1984). *Inviting school success: A self-concept approach to teaching and learning* (second edition). Belmont: Wadsworth.

Quirk, M. J. (1991). Indulging the liberal self: Richard Rorty's public voices. *Tikkun, 6*(3), 37–42 and 93–94.

Raitz, K. L. (1989). Detached technique and expert systems: Dead end for the effective teaching movement? In *Philosophy Of Education: 1988*, 50–61. Normal: Philosophy of Education Society.

Reiman, Jeffrey H. (1976). Privacy, intimacy, and personhood. *Philosophy & Public Affairs* 6:1 (Fall), 26–44. Reprinted in F. D. Shoeman (Ed). (1984), *Philosophical dimensions of privacy*, 300–316. Cambridge: Cambridge University Press. Page references are to the latter.

Reynolds, J. (1966). Children's privacy within the school context. In F. T. Villemain (Ed.) *Philosophy of Education 1966: Proceedings of the Twenty-Second Annual Meeting of the Philosophy of Education Society*, 255–263. Edwardsville: Philosophy of Education Society (Published by *Studies in Philosophy and Education*).

Ricard, F. (1987). Satan's point of view: Toward a reading of *Life is elsewhere. Salmagundi, 73*, 58–64.

Rice, S. & Burbules, N. C. (1993). Communicative virtues and educational relations. In H. Alexander (Ed.), *Philosophy of Education 1992*, 34–44. Champaign: Philosophy of Education Society.

Rorty, R. (1982). *Consequences of pragmatism*. Minneapolis: University of Minnesota Press.

Rorty, R. (1989). Education without dogma. *Dissent*, Spring, 198–206.

Rorty, R. (1991). *Essays on Heidegger and others.* Cambridge: Cambridge University Press.

Rorty, R. (1991). Habermas and Lyotard on postmodernity. In *Essays on Heidegger and Others,* 164–176. Cambridge: Cambridge University Press.

Rud, A. (1992). Building a rationale for teacher renewal. In Rud, A. & Oldendorf, W. (Eds.), *A place for teacher renewal: Challenging the intellect, creating educational reform,* 45–62. New York: Teachers College Press.

Rud, A., & Oldendorf, W. (Eds.). (1992). *A place for teacher renewal: Challenging the intellect, creating educational reform.* New York: Teachers College Press.

Russell, B. (1935; 1968). *Religion and science.* Oxford: Oxford University Press.

Saddhatissa, H. (1976). *The life of the Buddha.* New York: Harper and Row.

Sandel, M. (1982). *Liberalism and the limits of justice.* Cambridge: Harvard University Press.

Sarason, S. (1990). *The predictable failure of educational reform: Can we change course before it's too late?* San Francisco: Jossey-Bass.

Schacht, R. (1980). Nietzsche and nihilism. In R. Solomon (Ed.), *Nietzsche: A Collection of Critical Essays,* 58–82. Notre Dame: University of Notre Dame Press.

Schön, D. (1983). *The reflective practitioner: How professionals think in action.* New York: Basic Books.

Seery, J. (1990). *Political returns: Irony in politics and theory from Plato to the antinuclear movement.* Boulder: Westview Press.

Sheridan, A. (1980). *Michel Foucault: The will to truth.* New York: Tavistock.

Shulman, L. S. (1987a). Knowledge and teaching: foundations of the new reform. *Harvard Educational Review, 57*(1), 1–22.

Shulman, L. S. (1987b). Sounding an alarm: A reply to Sockett. *Harvard Educational Review, 57*(4), 473–482.

Sirotnik, K. (1991). Society, schooling, teaching, and preparing to teach. In Goodlad, J., Soder, R., and Sirotnik, K., *The moral dimensions of teaching,* 296–327. San Francisco: Jossey-Bass.

Sockett, H. (1987). Has Shulman got the strategy right? *Harvard Educational Review, 57*(2), 208–219.

Sockett, H. (1989). Research, practice, and professional aspiration within teaching. *Journal of Curriculum Studies 21,* 97–112.

Sockett, H. (1991). Accountability, trust, and ethical codes of practice. In Goodlad, J., Soder, R., & Sirotnik, K., *The moral dimensions of teaching,* 224–250. San Francisco: Jossey-Bass.

Sockett, H. (1992). Luck, excellence, and accountability in teaching: A reply to Shirley Pendlebury. In M. Buchmann and R. Floden (Eds.), *Philosophy of education 1991*, 71–74. Normal: Philosophy of Education Society.

Suzuki, D. T. (1970). *The field of Zen.* New York: Harper & Row.

Task Force on Education for Economic Growth (1983). *Action for excellence.* Denver, CO: Education Commission of the State.

Taylor, F. W. (1911). *The principles of scientific management.* New York: Harper & Row.

The Holmes Group (1986). *Tomorrow's teachers.* East Lansing.

The Holmes Group (1990). *Tomorrow's schools: Principles for the design of professional development schools.* East Lansing.

The Public Information Network (1985). *Equity and excellence: Toward an agenda for school reform.* St. Louis.

The Twentieth Century Fund (1983). *Making the grade: Report of the twentieth century fund task force on federal elementary and secondary education policy.* New York.

Thoreau, H. (1854; 1983). *Walden.* New York: Penguin.

Tom, A. R. (1984). *Teaching as a moral craft.* New York: Longman.

Tredennick, H. (1959). *The last days of Socrates: Euthyphro, Apology, Crito, and Phaedo.* Harmonsworth: Penguin.

Tyack, D. (1974). *The one best system: A history of American urban education.* Cambridge: Harvard University Press.

van Manen, M. (1982). Edifying theory: Serving the good. *Theory into Practice, 21*(1), 44–49.

van Manen, M. (1991). *The tact of teaching: The meaning of pedagogical thoughtfulness.* Albany: State University of New York Press.

Vince, R. W. (1984). *Ancient and medieval theatre: A historiographical handbook.* Westport: Greenwood Press. Taken from Vitruvius (1931; 1970). *On Architecture.* (trans. F. Granger). Cambridge: Harvard University Press.

Vlastos, G. (1991). *Socrates: Ironist and moral philosopher.* Ithaca: Cornell University Press.

White, P. (1986). Self-respect, self-esteem, and the school: A democratic perspective on authority. *Teachers College Record, 88*(1), 95–106.

Whitehead, A. N. (1929; 1967). The aims of education. In *The Aim of Education and Other Essays.* New York: The Free Press.

Wiggins, D. (1980). Deliberation and practical reason. In A. O. Rorty (Ed.), *Essays on Aristotle's Ethics*, 221–240. Berkeley: University of California Press.

Wilde, A. (1981). *Horizons of assent: Modernism, postmodernism, and the ironic imagination.* Baltimore: Johns Hopkins University Press.

Williams, B. (1981). *Moral luck: Philosophical papers 1973–1980.* Cambridge: Cambridge University Press.

Wilshire, B. W. (1984). *William James: The essential writings.* Albany: State University of New York Press.

Wirth, A. G. (1980). *Education in the technological society.* New York: University Press of America.

Wirth, A. G. (1983). *Productive work in industry and schools: Becoming persons again.* Lanham: University Press of America.

Wirth, A. G. (1992). *Education and work for the year 2000: Choice we face.* San Francisco: Jossey-Bass.

Wise, A. E. (1979). *Legislated learning: The bureaucratization of the American classroom.* Berkeley: University of California Press.

Wise, A. E. (1988). The two conflicting trends in school reform: Legislated learning revisited. *Phi Delta Kappan, 69*(5), 328–333.

Wittgenstein, L. (1953). *Philosophical investigations.* Oxford: Basil Blackwell.

Wittgenstein, L. (1969). *On certainty.* New York: Harper & Row.

Wolin, S. S. (1990). Democracy in the discourse of postmodernism. *Social Research, 57*(1), 5–29.

Zeichner, K. & Gore, J. (1990). Teacher socialization. In *Handbook of Research on Teacher Education,* 329–348. W. R. Houston (Ed.) New York: Macmillan.

Zeichner, K. & Liston, D. (1990). *Traditions of reform and reflective teaching in U.S. teacher education* (issue paper 90–91). East Lansing: National Center for Research on Teacher Education.

Index